D0484170

Veggie Planet

Uncover the Vegan Treasures Hiding in Your Favorite World Cuisines

Written by Wendy Werneth

www.thenomadicvegan.com

Veggie Planet: Uncover the Vegan Treasures Hiding in Your Favorite World Cuisines

Copyright © 2017 by **Wendy Werneth**

All rights reserved.

Published by Nomadic Vegan Publishing 2017

Lisbon, Portugal

This book is licensed for your personal enjoyment only. Feel free to share it – just don't try to pass it off as your own! If you enjoy this book, I really hope you'll do me the favor of leaving a review. You can connect with me at www.thenomadicvegan.com

Book and cover design by Derek Murphy

For more information, write to
wendy@thenomadicvegan.com.

ISBN-13: 978-1547296064

ISBN-10: 1547296062

Free Bonuses Package

Not everything I want to share with you can fit into a paperback book format. In order to make the contents of Veggie Planet as useful and practical for you as possible, I have created a package of additional bonuses that I'm offering to you for free. The bonuses include full color photos of the dishes described in the book, as well as downloadable pocket guides that you can bring with you to restaurants when traveling or eating out.

To claim your bonuses, go to:

thenomadicvegan.com/veggieplanetbonuses

Contents

Chapter One

The World is More Vegan-Friendly than You Think

When you hear the word "vegan", what first comes to your mind? Do you picture an abundance and huge variety of delicious foods? Most people don't, and just a few years ago I certainly didn't either. There is a commonly held view that a vegan diet and lifestyle is limiting and restrictive.

I understand why people think this way because I once held the same misconception. This is especially common among those of us who come from a culture where meat is traditionally the focus of every meal. In the United States and other English-speaking countries, vegetables are eaten as side dishes, if at all, and are not considered to be a meal on their own.

This is seen in common expressions like "meat and potatoes" or "meat and two veg" that are used to describe the standard American or British meal. A plate of mushy peas and mashed potatoes for dinner doesn't sound very appetizing, does it?

People who grew up eating this way often assume that vegans only eat boring side dishes or salads, because in their culinary tradition these are the only parts of the meal that are vegan.

But in other cultures, the composition of dishes is very different. There are many culinary traditions around the world where meat and other animal products are used sparingly, primarily for flavoring, while vegetables, grains, and legumes are the real stars of the meal.

The world is full of delicious plant-based dishes just waiting to be discovered, and I don't want you to miss out on them. That's why I wrote this book - to help you uncover the hidden vegan treasures that have been right there under your nose all along, in all your favorite world cuisines.

Maybe you've been vegan for many years already, or maybe you're just curious and want to dip your toes in and try out this healthy and compassionate way of eating.

Maybe you have no intention of becoming vegan, but you'd like to incorporate more nutritious, plant-based meals into your life. Or you're interested in world cuisines and would like to explore them from a different viewpoint.

Whatever it was that led you to pick up this book, I can promise that you're going to learn a great deal from it. If you currently think of veganism as a form of deprivation and restriction, this book will flip that belief on its head.

And if you are already enjoying the many benefits of a vegan lifestyle, you will enjoy them even more after discovering new ingredients, new dishes, and even new cultures within the pages of this book.

One by one, I'm going to introduce you to 11 of the most vegan-friendly cuisines on the planet. We're about to set off on a round-the-world foodie journey, so get your taste buds ready for a voyage of discovery! You'll be amazed at the variety of vegan dishes in these cuisines.

While you're probably familiar with at least a few of these 11 world cuisines already, I bet you haven't tried all the delicious vegan dishes they offer. By taking another look at these cuisines through a vegan lens, you'll rediscover them and come to appreciate them on a whole new level.

Some of these cuisines have a reputation of being very meat-heavy and therefore bad options for vegans and vegetarians. But that's not true at all!

While there certainly are meat-based dishes in these cuisines, and while those are often the dishes that are highlighted in guidebooks and on restaurant menus, there are plenty more specialties that are also part of the local culinary tradition but are not as well known outside the country where the cuisine was created. And many of these dishes are vegan or can easily be veganized.

When you finish this book, you will be confident in your ability to find a delicious vegan meal anywhere you go. No more nightmarish thoughts about subsisting on salad and French fries. Instead, you'll be full of excitement and anticipation about all the new tastes and flavors that await you.

You'll be eagerly planning your next trip to a destination you'd never considered before. Or, if international travel is not in the cards for you right now, you'll be checking your local restaurant listings for the address of the nearest Ethiopian or Vietnamese restaurant.

I don't expect you to book flights to all 11 of the countries discussed in this book, of course. The beauty of these cuisines is that, in most cases, you won't have to travel far to enjoy them! I have purposefully chosen only cuisines that have been exported well beyond the borders of the countries where they originated and are now served in restaurants all over the world.

This means that no matter where you may be traveling to, you will most likely find a restaurant nearby that serves one of these cuisines. Perhaps you're not planning to travel at all, and you just want to be able to eat out in your own town or city and enjoy a delicious, plant-based meal.

You can absolutely do that! Even if you live in a fairly small town, there are probably dozens of vegan options in your local restaurants. And after reading this book you will know exactly which types of restaurants to eat at and which dishes to look for on the menu.

You might even find yourself searching for recipes so you can recreate the delicious flavors of these cuisines in your own kitchen. I'll also tell you exactly where to find mouthwatering vegan recipes so that you can do just that.

So, how did I discover all these little-known vegan treasures from around the world? Well, when I first began researching vegan travel, I thought I was teaching myself a "survival skill". As I mentioned earlier, I had a lot of misconceptions and false beliefs about veganism, and I definitely did not imagine that a vegan lifestyle would be filled with an abundance and huge variety of delicious, healthy foods. No meat, fish, dairy or eggs? But I ate those things at practically every meal! What on earth would I eat as a vegan?

And as an avid traveler with a passion for exploring remote corners of the world, I was especially concerned about how I would maintain a vegan lifestyle while traveling. Travel is my first love; I fantasized about it even as a young child while looking through picture books of famous world monuments like the Taj Mahal and the Dome of the Rock with my Dad. I didn't realize then that it would become my full-time lifestyle, but once I finally left home after college and started traveling I found that I didn't want to stop.

When I boarded that first plane for France in March 1999, I set out on what I thought was going to be a six-month stint in Europe. Six months came and went, and then another six, and eventually I realized that I never wanted to go home. So I didn't.

For the past 18 years, I've been living, working and traveling in different places around the world. I've stepped foot on all seven continents, and I just recently visited my 100th country! Most people who know me think that I've already been everywhere there is to go, but that's not true at all. At current count, there are 196 countries in the world, which means I'm barely halfway there!

There are still plenty of places left that I plan to visit. I'm not done with travel now, and I definitely wasn't done with it back when I was first contemplating the possibility of becoming vegan. And so, my love for travel held me back from taking my vegan journey all the way. I was sure that being vegan would ruin travel, and I didn't really believe it would be possible to stay vegan in some of the places I intended to visit.

I imagined that vegan travel would mean creating lots of stress and hassle for myself and eating lots of tasteless, unhealthy meals of French fries and ketchup. Or white rice and soy sauce, depending on which part of the world I was traveling in.

And yet, the more I learned about the massive environmental destruction caused by the meat and dairy industries, the harmful effects that animal products were having on my own health, and the terrible suffering of the animals who are raised for their flesh, milk, and eggs, the more I was convinced that adopting a vegan lifestyle was the only way that I could find inner peace and live in alignment with my own values.

And so, on a three-week trip to Greece, I decided to give veganism a trial run. I figured that if I was able to stay vegan throughout that whole trip, then I would have to admit that vegan travel was, in fact, possible.

Imagine how pleasantly surprised I was to find that traditional Greek cuisine is full of naturally vegan dishes! Every day I experienced new flavors and new ingredients that I had never tried before. It seemed that each time I picked up a restaurant menu, there was a new vegan dish to try.

I still carried around an emergency stash of granola bars and other snacks, just in case. Gradually, though, I came to realize that even that sensible precaution wasn't really necessary. There was absolutely no chance that I was going to get stuck somewhere and have to go hungry for lack of any vegan options.

Once I had learned a little bit about the local cuisine, I could see that every single restaurant I walked into had not just one, but several vegan dishes on offer. My trip turned into a kind of treasure hunt, as each day I stayed on the lookout for new vegan discoveries. And I kept finding them!

I was discovering the local cuisine and connecting with the local culture in a way that most other visitors weren't. I would sometimes listen to the tourists at the table next to me place their order. I could see that they were staying well within their comfort zone, sticking faithfully to the handful of standard "local specialties" that they'd read about in their guidebook and knew how to pronounce.

Meanwhile, I was rattling off the names of Greek dishes that they had never heard of before and uncovering the real, authentic Greek cuisine - the foods that Greek families have been enjoying together for centuries.

As I learned more about the history of Greek cuisine and the reasons why it includes so many vegan options, I also gained fascinating cultural insights that are completely unknown to most visitors. Much to my surprise, being vegan had not made travel worse. In fact, it had made travel even better.

From that moment on, I never looked back. The day my plane touched down in Athens - September 10th, 2014 - is the day that I celebrate as my veganniversary. Since that day, I have traveled to many more countries as a vegan, and I've learned along the way that Greece is not an anomaly. There are vegan treasures hiding in every single world cuisine.

In addition to my travels, I've also done plenty of exploration in my own kitchen at home. Actually, just stepping foot in the kitchen could almost be considered a type of exploration for me, because before going vegan I never cooked. And I really mean *never* cooked. I could pour milk into a bowl of cereal, and that was the extent of my meal preparation skills.

And while my husband still holds the title of head chef in our family, I now genuinely enjoy puttering around in the kitchen, which is something I would never have imagined myself doing.

Contrary to what I had imagined, becoming vegan has actually expanded my culinary horizons. I eat a much wider variety of foods than I did before, and being vegan has led me to the discovery of so many new tastes and flavor combinations that I would never have known about otherwise.

And I know I'm not the only one that has experienced this kind of discovery. Most vegans I talk to say the same thing - they enjoy food so much more now as vegans than they did in their pre-vegan days. Many of them have discovered entire cuisines thanks to their newfound interest in plant-based eating. I know quite a few vegans who had never tried Ethiopian food before but then fell head over heels in love with it after adopting a vegan lifestyle.

In my case, my world travels had already introduced me to many different ethnic cuisines. And yet, as a vegan, I've rediscovered those cuisines all over again. I've come to realize just how much more they have to offer. Even though I had previously traveled for weeks and even months at a time in the countries where those cuisines were created, in all that time I had barely scratched the surface.

Being vegan has given me a newfound appreciation for food and food culture, and it has opened up a window through which I can explore the places I visit at a much deeper and more meaningful level. In addition, it has also given me the inner peace that comes with living in a way that is in line with my own values of compassion, peace, and non-violence. My only regret is that I didn't make the change sooner.

I can't wait to show you the abundance of treasures hiding in all these vegan-friendly cuisines from around the world. But before we go any further, let's take a closer look at two of the words in that last sentence: **"abundance"** and **"vegan-friendly"**.

These words will be popping up many times in this book, so it's important that you understand what I mean when I use them. Before we set off on our culinary tour around the world, let's first take a moment to define these two terms.

Two Key Concepts: "Vegan-Friendly" and "Abundance"

What is Vegan-Friendly?

First, let's talk about the term "vegan-friendly". A country, city or any other geographical area can be "vegan-friendly" in one of two ways.

Vegan-Friendly by Demand

The type of vegan-friendly destination that you are probably most familiar with is the type where there is an abundance of vegan options because the vegan movement itself is strong there.

In the United States, for example, Portland, Oregon; Austin, Texas; and Asheville, North Carolina are all cities that have reputations as being vegan-friendly. In Europe, the English seaside town of Brighton is known for its many vegetarian and vegan restaurants, and Berlin is often touted as the vegan capital of the world.

Again, this is because there are large vegan communities living in these cities. Those communities have created a demand for vegan options, and local businesses have responded to that demand.

In this type of vegan-friendly destination, you will likely see restaurant signs and menus advertising the fact that the establishment offers vegan dishes. Restaurants and other eateries will proudly display their vegan-friendly credentials because they are trying to draw in potential customers who are looking for vegan food.

Vegan-Friendly by Accident

The second type of vegan-friendly destination - the one we're going to be focusing on in this book - is much less obvious. Consequently, these destinations are often mistakenly thought to be difficult places for vegetarians and vegans to travel.

I've even heard vegans describe some of the countries featured in this book as a "vegan wasteland" or a "vegan culinary desert". Nothing could be further from the truth! It really saddens me to think that these people missed out on so much delicious food, simply because they didn't know what to ask for or how to ask for it.

I was browsing an online forum on vegan travel recently, and one visitor to China said that she had been in the country for 10 days and that she had only been able to eat two meals that whole time. I have no idea what she did for food at all the other meal times, but it sounds like she had a pretty miserable trip.

I don't want that to happen to you! Which is why I've written this book. You see, in order to get the most out of this second type of vegan-friendly destination, you really need to have the right resources at hand.

These destinations don't wear their vegan-friendly credentials on their sleeve. Instead, visitors will need to scratch below the surface to uncover the vegan treasures these places have to offer.

This is because this second type of vegan-friendly destination has a traditional cuisine that is naturally vegan-friendly and that has been around long before the term "vegan" was ever coined. You might also call this type of cuisine "accidentally vegan-friendly".

In some countries, this is a result of geography and climate, while in others it is the result of long-standing religious traditions that have been followed for centuries or even millennia. In the case of religiously influenced cuisines, the term "accidentally vegan-friendly" is perhaps not entirely accurate.

Buddhist and Hindu traditions, for example, are based on a creed of non-violence and respect for all sentient beings, so the fact that they eschew most or all animal products is no accident.

But regardless of whether the locals avoid meat because they revere cows as sacred or because their land is simply unsuitable for grazing, restaurants in these types of destinations are much less likely to slap a "Vegan OK" sticker on their menu. In fact, it's quite possible that they've never even heard the word "vegan" before.

For this reason, when visiting these places you can't rely on locals to advertise their vegan options. You'll need to do a little bit of research to uncover them. But don't worry, I've done all the research for you. With this book in hand, you'll know exactly what to ask for.

In the upcoming chapters, we will explore 11 of the world's most vegan-friendly cuisines. All of these cuisines fall into the second of the two vegan-friendly categories I've just described. This is the food eaten by locals in countries where the culinary tradition naturally includes many vegan dishes.

This Is NOT All There Is

This does not mean that these 11 are the *only* vegan-friendly cuisines in the world. Far from it. All across the globe, there are plenty more cuisines that are largely plant-based. In fact, traditionally, before the invention of modern industrial agriculture, most human societies ate a diet that was heavily focused on plants.

As I've already mentioned, the reason why I've chosen to highlight these 11 cuisines in particular is because they are widely available not only in the countries where they originated but all around the world.

Immigrants from these countries have opened restaurants all across the globe, thereby spreading their cuisine far and wide. This means that when choosing a travel destination, you don't have to limit yourself to one of these 11 countries in order to enjoy these plant-based dishes.

In fact, you'll find a restaurant serving at least one of these cuisines just about anywhere in the world. No matter where you are traveling, if you find a restaurant specializing in one of these cuisines, you are almost certain to find a variety of delicious vegan options.

So just because your next travel destination is not featured in this book, don't let that scare you. It may be that the food eaten in your country of choice is just as vegan-friendly as these 11 cuisines but is simply not widely known outside that country.

To show you what I mean, let's take just a few examples from different parts of the world. The Caribbean island of Trinidad boasts an Indian-influenced cuisine that is just bursting with the flavors of stewed chickpeas, sweet chutneys, and peppery sauces.

Georgia (the country, not the US state) also has a plethora of naturally vegan dishes, such as stewed kidney beans, eggplant rolls topped with walnut paste, and mushroom-or-potato-filled soup dumplings.

To give just one more example, the local cuisine eaten in the East African country of Uganda features beans, peanut sauces, plantains, rice and root vegetables, not to mention all the fresh fruit and fruit juices that are found in abundance.

I hope that one day I'll be able to write a whole book about each one of these cuisines, but for now, we're just going to focus on the ones that are the most popular on a global scale.

11 Cuisines You Can Find Anywhere

These are the ones that will come in handy no matter where you are. Because at some point, you may find yourself in a country or region that is most definitely *not* vegan-friendly. Perhaps you are living in a place like this right now.

Let's take France, for example. I hear a lot of complaints from vegan travelers about how difficult it is to find vegan food in France. And I'll admit that French cuisine, in the north of the country, in particular, is very much centered on meat and dairy products.

That doesn't mean that it's impossible to get a vegan meal in a typical French restaurant. On the contrary, I've been pleasantly surprised on a number of occasions by French chefs who have used their creativity to whip up a gorgeous, vegetable-based meal just for me, even though there was nothing remotely vegan listed on the menu.

But let's say that, for whatever reason, you don't want to ask for a special meal. Well, then you don't have to!

All you have to do is ignore the traditional French restaurants and instead seek out a restaurant that specializes in one of the cuisines featured in this book. This won't be hard to do, because these are the most popular cuisines in the world.

Chinese and Moroccan restaurants in particular can be seen on just about every street corner in Paris.

Granted, sometimes the exported versions of these cuisines - the ones that you find in immigrant-run restaurants *outside* the country where the cuisine originated - are a bit different from the more authentic, original version.

For this reason, each chapter of this book is divided into three sections. In the first section, we will explore the cuisine in its original form - the way it's prepared in the country that created it. If you are visiting one of these countries, this is the section that you'll want to pay the closest attention to.

The second section will include descriptions of dishes in that cuisine that are naturally vegan or can easily be veganized upon request. Again, if you are heading to the country that invented the cuisine, you will definitely want to keep an eye out for these dishes.

This doesn't mean that these are the *only* vegan dishes in the cuisine. Far from it! This book is just meant to give you a general overview of the kinds of dishes you can expect to find. In the future, I will be publishing a "Veggie Lovers" series of books that explore individual cuisines in much greater depth.

The first book in the series will be *Italy for Veggie Lovers*, which will be published in 2018. If you'd like to be notified as soon as *Italy for Veggie Lovers* is released, sign up for updates at thenomadicvegan.com/veganitaly and I'll make sure that you're the first to know. I'll also send you a free sample chapter.

And lastly, the third section of each chapter will provide tips for eating in restaurants that serve the cuisine elsewhere in the world. If you are traveling to a country that's not covered in this book, or if you are looking for vegan-friendly restaurants near where you live, then this section will be particularly useful for you.

Some of the cuisines featured will be more familiar to you than others. While the book will probably introduce you to a few cuisines that you don't know very much about, it will also help you rediscover cuisines that you thought you already knew, and that you've been eating your whole life.

Odds are, your all-time favorite cuisine is one that's featured in this book. Even if you've been eating that type of food for decades, I'm willing to bet that you'll still learn something new about it, and perhaps discover a whole range of dishes that you never knew existed.

Don't Sweat the Small Stuff

You may be thinking to yourself, "But how do I know these dishes are *really* vegan? How can I be sure there aren't any hidden non-vegan ingredients?"

The answer is, unless you made the dish yourself, you can never be 100 percent sure about what's in it. So just do the best you can and then let it go.

In some cases, it's not always easy to determine whether a food is completely devoid of all animal-based ingredients. A seemingly plant-based lentil soup might be made with mutton broth, or it might have butter added to it. A tofu and vegetable stir-fry might be flavored with fish sauce or shrimp paste.

But before we go any further, perhaps first we should get clear about what is and is not vegan. According to the definition put forward by The Vegan Society, veganism is:

"a philosophy and way of living which seeks to exclude--as far as is possible and practicable--all forms of exploitation of, and cruelty to, animals for food, clothing or any other purpose".

This means avoiding cruelty and exploitation in all areas of our lives, not just in relation to what we put in our mouths. But since the subject of this book is world cuisines, we will limit our discussion here to which foods are vegan, and which foods aren't.

Basically, any food that does not contain meat, fish, eggs, dairy products or honey can be considered vegan. To put it another way, vegans don't eat animals or anything that comes out of an animal. Instead, they eat plants.

The members of The Vegan Society who first coined the term more than 70 years ago chose this lifestyle for ethical reasons, because they didn't want to cause any unnecessary suffering for animals. For myself and many of the vegans I know personally, this moral value of compassion for animals remains our primary motivation.

That's not to say that every vegan is a member of some secret society or exclusive club, though. The vegan movement is growing at a rapid pace and is attracting people from all walks of life who choose to become vegan for a variety of different reasons. For some, their main motivation is to drastically reduce their impact on the environment by eating in a way that is more sustainable than the standard Western diet.

Others are introduced to the lifestyle through the many health benefits of a plant-based diet. They have discovered that, by eating whole, plant foods, it's possible to prevent, treat, and even reverse many of the chronic diseases afflicting our society, such as diabetes, heart disease, Alzheimer's, and even some forms of cancer.

And in recent years, a number of professional athletes who compete in sports ranging from figure skating to bodybuilding to ultra-marathon running have adopted a plant-based diet. These athletes have found that eating this way improves their performance and aids in their recovery during training.

Regardless of their motivation for adopting a vegan lifestyle, all of these vegans have one thing in common: they are trying their best to avoid consuming any animal products.

In theory, this sounds straightforward, but in reality, the use and exploitation of animals are so entrenched in our society that it's virtually impossible to live in the modern world and completely avoid contact with all animal products.

There are so many bones, ears, hoofs and other unwanted body parts left over from the slaughter of billions of animals every year, that slaughterhouses have come up with ingenious ways of turning these into "by-products" that end up in all kinds of consumer goods, both edible and non-edible.

Some vegans do make it their mission to uncover any minute quantity of animal flesh or bodily secretions that might sneak its way into their food. They memorize the E-numbers used for food additives in Europe, for example, and avoid any packaged foods that contain E542 (edible bone phosphate) or E120 (a red food coloring made from the crushed bodies of insects), among others.

And while I certainly understand the desire to avoid contributing to any animal suffering, I personally take a more relaxed approach, mainly because I'm concerned that obsessing over minute quantities of animal products may ultimately cause more harm than good.

Rather than attempting to achieve some kind of personal purity, I'm much more interested in making veganism an attractive lifestyle that others want to follow. I am vegan for many reasons, but the main motivational force that drives all the work that I do is my desire to spare as many animals as possible from unnecessary suffering.

And if I can influence just one other person's decision to become vegan, or to become vegetarian, or even to just reduce their meat intake by half, that's still going to spare many more animals' lives than fine-tuning my own diet to eliminate that final 1 percent of animal products.

If, every time I go out to eat, I start grilling the waiter about the contents of my bread roll before I even look at the menu, then he and everyone else around me is going to think that vegans are annoying, obsessive, fanatic, extremist, or any other negative adjective you can think of.

By making vegans and veganism look difficult, I am actually discouraging other people from adopting a vegan lifestyle. Which of course is the exact opposite of what I want to do!

That's why, personally, I don't worry too much about hidden ingredients like meat stock or lard. Each individual has to decide where to draw their vegan line, though, and not everyone is going to agree on what is possible and practicable. There are also some people who would become physically ill if they ate these things, even in small quantities. If that's your situation, then, of course, you will want to be more attentive about exactly what goes into your food.

With this in mind, I've created a tool that you can use to inquire about possible non-vegan ingredients if you want to.

If you go to henomadicvegan.com/veggieplanetbonuses, you will find a list of non-vegan ingredients that are commonly used in the cuisines discussed in this book, even if it's usually in small amounts (e.g. a tablespoon of fish sauce or a teaspoon of shrimp paste).

The list includes a short description of each ingredient and an explanation of how each one is typically used and which dishes it's most likely to be found in. It's up to you to decide just how vigilant you want to be about avoiding these ingredients.

And if, despite your best efforts, one of those ingredients *does* end up in your dish, don't beat yourself up over it. Being vegan is not about being perfect. Nobody is perfect. Being vegan is simply about doing the best you can to cause the least harm.

What is Abundance?

Now that we've established what "vegan-friendly" means, let's talk about the word "abundance". You might be wondering how this word is relevant to the subject of this book. Well, the truth is, if you want to benefit from this book at all, it's absolutely essential that you understand the concept of abundance.

The word "abundance" is often associated with financial wealth, but it's about much more than having a lot of money.

In fact, the pursuit of more money is *not* the road to abundance.

Abundance is a mentality, a state of mind. In order to experience abundance in our lives, we have to develop an abundance consciousness so that we can connect with the abundance that already surrounds us.

Now if that sounds too woo-woo or new age, then instead of cultivating an "abundance consciousness", just think about this as cultivating a "positive attitude". Essentially, having an abundance mindset is simply a matter of approaching life with a positive attitude.

And this attitude will be key to your enjoyment of food, travel, and all other aspects of life. I'm going to use a real-life example to show you what I mean about abundance consciousness, and also how it relates to vegan food.

Recently, in an online group about vegan travel, a member made a couple of posts asking people to list what they had found to be the easiest and the hardest places to be vegan. Want to know the answers? OK, let's play a little guessing game.

Below, you'll find a list of countries. Take a look at the list and decide which ones you think were voted as the hardest places to be vegan, and which were voted as the easiest:

China

India

Thailand

Greece

Italy

France

Have you divided these up into "easiest" and "hardest" buckets yet? Don't move on to the next paragraph until you have your answers ready. Which ones do you think were among the easiest vegan travel destinations?

The correct answer is all of them! All of these destinations were mentioned by at least one group member as being the easiest place to find vegan food that they'd ever visited. So then, which ones were voted as the hardest places to be vegan?

Once again, the answer is all of them! But how is this possible? How can vegan travelers have such vastly different experiences in these countries?

There are several factors that could have contributed to this, but the most important one is this: some of the travelers were experiencing life with an abundance mindset, and others were going through life with a scarcity mindset.

Here's one example of a vegan traveler with a scarcity mindset. I won't use his name here, but this is what he wrote on a public forum about his travels in Greece:

"A few months ago I went to Greece for 4 months and it was a vegan wasteland. Greeks have a close minded mentality so outside of Athens you cannot really find international cuisine that might be vegan. Also there is a noveau-rich (sic) mentality despite the crisis there so progressive causes like bicycling, vegetarianism and veganism are far behind the rest of the West. People there rather display wealth and dominance, even more so than the USA."

Now, in the chapter on Greek cuisine, I will tell you all about the amazing variety of vegan dishes in Greece, as well as the cultural aspects that have led to such a vegan-friendly cuisine. I won't go into all of that right now, but let's just say that "vegan wasteland" is the most inappropriate term I can possibly imagine to describe Greece.

I responded to this traveler's post and tried to politely let him know that Greek food is abundant in vegan dishes. Well, guess what? He already knew that.

It turns out that he's a second-generation Greek-American who speaks and reads Greek fluently and has family members who live in Greece. He knew perfectly well how to ask for the many traditional dishes in Greek cuisine that are naturally vegan.

But did that mean he enjoyed his trip? Clearly not. His knowledge of Greek cuisine didn't help him one bit. The vegan abundance in Greece was still invisible to him. He wasn't looking for abundance; he was looking for scarcity and lack. And that's exactly what he found.

That's why it's so important that you and I talk about abundance first, before I tell you about the amazing vegan dishes in all these world cuisines.

Because if you're stuck in a scarcity mindset, then the rest of the information in this book is not going to help you. A scarcity mindset is the belief that there is a shortage or scarcity of good things in life, whether it's money, love, food or anything else. This creates fear and an internal conversation in your head that says "there's not enough for me".

In order to experience and enjoy the abundance that surrounds you, you have to move past those fears and negative thoughts by telling your brain to focus on something else. You see, you are constantly surrounded by and bombarded with all different kinds of stimuli, including sights, smells, sounds, and tastes. Your brain would be completely overwhelmed if it tried to take in all these stimuli, so instead it just focuses on what you tell it to focus on and ignores the rest.

There is a part of your brain called the reticular activating system that acts as a filter for the constant barrage of sights, sounds, tastes, and colors that you are faced with every second of the day. Your brain can't process all of this at once, so your reticular activating system's job is to only let through the things that it thinks are important.

And how does it know what's important? By what you focus on the most. Be very careful about what you focus on, because depending on what your focus is, you are training your brain to either work for you or against you. If you focus on the negative, your brain will filter out the positive and you'll never even know it was there.

Fortunately, there are some simple, easy practices that you can incorporate into your daily life to help you to reset your focus. The three that I have found to be the most effective in my own life are:

1. Keeping a gratitude journal

2. Repeating positive affirmations

3. Giving thanks on a regular basis

I've created a short guide for you that explains how I use these, and how you too can start using these practices today to create an abundance mindset. You can download your free guide at: thenomadicvegan.com/veggieplanetbonuses.

These practices won't take very long, and they will allow you to start seeing the abundance in your world that you may be missing right now. By changing your thoughts, you will change your life. Yep, your thoughts are *that powerful*.

Do you feel like you don't have control over your own thoughts? It's easy to allow ourselves to be swept along by the constant stream of chatter running through our heads.

I'm guilty of this too. I sometimes catch myself repeating old conversations over and over, instead of living in the moment and enjoying the world around me. When that happens, I look up at the blue sky and remember something I learned from Andy Puddicombe.

Andy is a meditation teacher and a former Buddhist monk, and he created the Headspace guided meditation app, which I use every day as part of my morning routine.

Andy says that your mind is like the blue sky - a blank canvas on which thoughts, feelings, and experiences appear. Usually these thoughts, feelings, and experiences are just little, wispy, white clouds, and you're not bothered or distracted by them too much. When you have a blue sky mind that's mostly clear, your mind is calm, serene and happy.

Sometimes, though, those clouds get bigger, darker, and more ominous, and you might even feel like there's a hurricane on its way. When this happens, it's easy to forget about the blue sky altogether. But it's still there! That underlying calm that we are looking for is already there; we just have to rise above the clouds to find it.

Think about the last time you flew in an airplane. What happened after takeoff? The plane climbed steadily up through the clouds, right? It might have been a bit bumpy and turbulent while you were passing through those clouds, but eventually you found yourself up above them. You were back in the blue sky that had been there all along.

So how do you find that blue sky inside yourself when your mind is filled with dark clouds? How do you reset your focus so that you can see the wonderful abundance that surrounds you?

Your brain is like a muscle, and you can train it to do what you want it to do. Just like the muscles in the rest of your body, your brain needs exercise. It needs to be trained to work for you instead of against you. Resetting your focus to create an abundance mindset is not a one-off thing. You can't just set it once and be done with it. It requires daily practice.

That sounds like a lot of hard work, and right now you may be thinking that I was lying when I said that these practices were simple and easy and wouldn't take up much of your time.

I wasn't lying; they *are* simple, quick and easy. But in the beginning they will probably feel like hard work, because you will be breaking out of your normal routine and telling your brain to do something that it's not used to doing.

We humans are resistant to change. It's so much easier to stick with the habits that we're familiar and comfortable with, even if we know that those habits are hurting us.

The first day of taking a new action is always the hardest. But every day that you do it, it becomes a little bit easier. And eventually, the action becomes your new habit, and you do it automatically without thinking about it.

Do you have to ask yourself every day whether or not you're going to brush your teeth? Do you have to psyche yourself up to pick up your toothbrush? Probably not. Brushing your teeth has become a habit for you, because you do it every day.

Now that you've created that habit, you reap the benefits of having clean and healthy teeth. And what's the price that you have to pay for that? Nothing. You don't have to agonize about whether or not you're going to do it, and you don't feel like you're wasting your time while you're doing it.

You know how great the benefits of brushing your teeth are, so you don't even consider whether there might be something better you could be doing with your time. You just do it.

If you put in some effort in the beginning to make these three daily practices a habit, then eventually they too will feel just like brushing your teeth. And how will they benefit you? They will help you to reset your focus, create an abundance mindset, and train your brain to work for you in as little as five minutes a day.

No matter how busy you are, I guarantee that you have five minutes in your day that could be better spent by doing these simple things to train your brain to work in your favor. And when you do, you're going to be amazed at the positive impact that these simple practices will have in your life.

Go to thenomadicvegan.com/veggieplanetbonuses now to claim your free guide that will show you how to use these practices to tap into the abundance that surrounds you.

What You Will Discover in This Book

All right, now that you have the tools you need to retrain your mind to focus on abundance, you're ready to experience the overwhelming abundance of vegan food that is out there waiting for you. In the following chapters, you will learn how to:

- Easily find a delicious vegan meal virtually anywhere in the world
- Order authentic local specialties that most tourists have never heard of
- Navigate restaurant menus and spot the hidden vegan treasures in them

You will also gain new insight into many different cultures around the world. The first culture and cuisine that we will start with is one that is at once familiar and unknown. I'm talking about Chinese cuisine.

According to Jennifer 8 Lee, author of *The Fortune Cookie Chronicles: Adventures in the World of Chinese Food*, the number of Chinese restaurants in the United States is larger than the number of McDonald's, Burger King and Wendy's restaurants combined.

And it's not only in the United States that Chinese restaurants are ubiquitous; Chinese immigrants have been prolific in opening up restaurants all over the world. There are about 250,000 Chinese people living in England, and 90 percent of them work in the restaurant business.

Odds are, you've eaten at least a few Chinese meals in your lifetime. But how much do you know about the *real* cuisine of China? We'll find out in the next chapter.

The World is More Vegan Friendly than You Think

Chapter Two

Chinese Cuisine

Vegan Food in China

Even though the word "vegan" was not coined until the mid-twentieth century in the United Kingdom, ancient China is, in some ways, the birthplace of veganism as a spiritual practice of non-violence towards all living beings.

While India is the true birthplace of several religious traditions that are based on the concept of non-violence (*ahimsa*), including Hinduism, Jainism, and Buddhism, the raising of cows for milk was - and still is - a key part of Indian culture. For that reason, while many people in India abstain from eating meat or eggs, milk products are widespread in Indian cuisine.

When Buddhist teachings were brought to China, however, those teachings were adapted in a way that resulted in a truly vegan diet for Chinese Buddhist monks. Unlike in neighboring Buddhist countries, where monks begged for alms and were obliged to eat whatever food they were given, Buddhist monks in ancient China actually produced their own food.

And, since the Buddha's teachings forbade the monks from killing any living being, in practice this meant that Chinese monks produced and ate only vegan food. While the monk's daily meals were made up of simple grains, vegetables, and legumes, they also learned to prepare richer dishes for visitors, such as the wealthy patrons who donated large sums to the monasteries.

Mock meats are nothing new, and they definitely didn't start with Tofurky. Chinese Buddhist monks invented seitan (面筋) back in the sixth century AD, and over the course of hundreds of years, they have refined the art of recreating the look, texture, and mouthfeel of meat-based dishes.

Even today, many Buddhist temples in China boast an attached restaurant, where you can taste vegan versions of popular meat-based dishes. The names of the dishes on the menu will probably contain the names of animals, such as "eel", "lobster" or "duck", but you can rest assured that these meats are made from plants.

Granted, most Chinese people today are not devout Buddhists and do not see any moral dilemma in the consumption of animal-based foods. Even so, the traditional Chinese diet has always been largely plant-based, with meat used in small quantities for flavoring. Many dishes that do contain meat can easily be prepared in meatless versions on request, either by simply omitting the meat or by substituting it with tofu, eggplant, mushrooms, etc.

Noodles, rice, tofu, and vegetables are all mainstays of Chinese cuisine. Nuts, water plants, and mushrooms and other fungi are also common ingredients. Also, the Chinese have been drinking soy milk for about 2,000 years.

Animal milk, on the other hand, was traditionally not consumed by most ethnic groups in China. In fact, the vast majority of Chinese people are lactose intolerant.

Given this culinary history, it's not surprising that Chinese cuisine boasts a huge number of naturally vegan specialties. And when I say huge, I mean hundreds, if not thousands of different dishes.

Food has always been of utmost importance in Chinese culture, and each region, city, and town in China takes pride in its local specialties. The food eaten in China changes radically from region to region, and the variety is astonishing.

When I moved to Beijing in 2008 to work for the organizing committee of the Beijing Olympic Games, I was exposed for the first time to many different Chinese regional cuisines. As you might expect, the Chinese capital is filled with thousands of restaurants run by migrants from the various regions, each serving the local specialties of their hometown.

Before arriving in China, I had been accustomed to making dinner plans with friends and being asked what kind of food I'd like to eat. Previously, my answers had always been something like, "I feel like Mexican tonight", or "I wouldn't mind going out for Indian".

With my Chinese friends in Beijing, though, I quickly learned that that was *not* the answer they were looking for. What they really meant when they asked that question was, "What kind of *Chinese* food would you like to eat?" Now of course, as a major world capital with a population of more than 20 million people, Beijing does have its fair share of Mexican and Indian restaurants, along with plenty of other eateries serving international food.

In my experience, though, even well-educated, upper-middle-class Beijingers are not all that familiar with these non-Chinese restaurants or the food they serve. They might try them out occasionally just to see what they're all about, but they would much prefer to visit a restaurant serving Chinese regional cuisine instead.

Perhaps this is because there is such huge variety within the regional cuisines of China. It's such a vast country that, by tasting the local specialties of Yunnan - which sits more than 1,300 miles (more than 2,000 kilometers) south of Beijing - they already feel like they are taking part in an exotic culinary experience. For the Chinese, regional cuisines are exotic, but still offer an underlying sense of familiarity. Unlike international cuisines, which are a bit *too* foreign.

Each regional cuisine is viewed as its own distinct type of food. Some regions like Sichuan and Hunan are known for favoring hot and spicy dishes, while others like Guangdong and Jiangsu have a lighter and sweeter flavor profile. When Chinese people travel to a different part of the country, tasting the local specialties there is an important part of the trip for them. And it can be for you too!

The dishes listed in the next section are just a very small sampling of the vast variety of dishes available in China. The ones that I have selected for inclusion here are commonly found in multiple regions of the country.

The name of each dish is given in pinyin (a system for writing Chinese using the Latin alphabet) as well as in simplified Chinese characters (the type of characters used throughout mainland China). To find out what the accents used in pinyin mean and how to pronounce them, see the Key Words and Phrases section at the end of this chapter.

Vegan or Veganizable Dishes to Seek Out

Bāozi - 包子 - Filled, steamed buns, often sold at street food stalls and eaten for breakfast or as a snack. Bāozi sellers are easily identified by the pile of steaming, round bamboo containers that the bāozi are cooked in. The general term for vegetable-filled bāozi is cài bāo (菜包), but occasionally these will also contain small bits of meat, so be sure to ask. For a sweet version of bāozi, try a dòu shā bāo (豆沙包), which is filled with sweet adzuki bean paste.

Dìsānxiān - 地三鲜 - Stir-fried eggplant, potato and bell peppers seasoned with chili and cooked in soy sauce and garlic. This is a northern specialty but is pretty widely available; I've even seen it on menus at some of the more authentic Chinese restaurants in Lisbon, Portugal. This dish is typically eaten with rice.

Málà dòufu - 麻辣豆腐 - Not to be confused with mápó dòufu (麻婆豆腐), which usually contains bits of minced meat, this tofu dish is served in a hot and spicy sauce and is usually eaten with rice.

Dòufu nǎo - 豆腐脑 - The name of this dish literally means "tofu brains", though it's also known by the more attractive name of "tofu flower" (dòufu huā (豆腐花)). This is a very soft form of tofu, almost like a pudding. It can be eaten as either a sweet or savory breakfast, depending on regional variations.

In the north of China, it's a savory dish seasoned with soy sauce and topped with pickled vegetables. In Sichuan, chili oil and Sichuan pepper are added to make it spicy, while in the south it's served with sweet ginger or syrup, sometimes with coconut milk added to it.

Pāihuángguā - 拍黄瓜 - Originally from Sichuan but now popular throughout China, this is a cold dish of cucumber mixed with sesame oil, minced garlic, cooking wine, soy sauce and vinegar. Sometimes small bits of red chili are also added. This is one of the few cold, uncooked salads you will find in China. Chinese people are generally adverse to eating raw foods, because Chinese medicine teaches that eating uncooked food is not good for one's health.

Yúxiāng qiézi - 鱼香茄子 - The name of this dish literally means "fish-flavor eggplant", but it doesn't contain any fish. The name just refers to the fact that the flavors in the sauce are normally thought to pair well with fish but are instead paired with a different ingredient.

The most popular (non-vegan) version of this dish is fish-flavor shredded pork (鱼香肉丝), but eggplant is also fairly common. If you see fish-flavor shredded pork on a menu, ask if they can make it with eggplant or tofu instead.

Shǒusī yuánbáicài - 手撕圆白菜 - Roughly-torn pieces of cabbage, fried and served with bits of hot chilies. A similar cabbage dish made with vinegar is known as cùliū báicài (醋溜白菜).

Básī - 拔丝 - If you have a sweet tooth, you'll love this northeastern dish of candied vegetables. It's usually made with pumpkin, or sometimes with potato. Eat it while it's hot and easy to pull apart; once it has cooled down the sweet mixture that coats the vegetables hardens and becomes difficult to eat! In some regions of China, this dish goes by the name of guàjiāng (挂浆).

Suānlà tǔdòusī - 酸辣土豆丝 - Finely shredded strips of potato in a hot and sour sauce. Don't imagine French fries; this is a much healthier dish. The potatoes are much thinner than French fries and are more like shoestring or matchstick potatoes in shape. Also, they are not fried.

Jīnzhēngū huángguā - 金针菇黄瓜 - In this dish, it is the cucumbers that are cut into long, thin shreds and then tossed with mushroom. This particular mushroom, which also has a long, thin shape, is known as the "golden needle mushroom" in Chinese (that's what 金针菇 means). In the West, it's more often known by its Japanese name: enoki mushroom.

But Will I Get Food Poisoning if I Eat This?

I've heard a number of people express concerns about food safety in China, so perhaps a quick word on the subject is in order. It's true that there have been several scandals in recent years involving the use of food additives and pesticides in China. The most notorious scandals have involved meat and other animal products (particularly cow's milk and milk-based baby formula), but plant-based foods can also be affected.

As always, be aware of the cleanliness of your food and take the necessary precautions. When traveling, it's usually not possible to know exactly how your food was produced, so you'll have to decide if you're willing to live with that uncertainty.

Personally, I'm willing to take a small risk if it means that I get to experience a new place and culture. I don't want to let fear stop me from fully experiencing everything the world has to offer.

I do take some precautions, such as drinking bottled water or, better yet, traveling with a water filter in places like China where the tap water is unsafe to drink. However, I still use unfiltered tap water to brush my teeth, and I eat raw fruits and vegetables that were probably washed in it. I also eat at street food stalls and other establishments where I know that the standard of hygiene is lower than what I would expect at home.

By avoiding meat and other animal products, I'm already at a lower risk of food poisoning than other travelers. Occasionally I do get sick from something I eat, but usually I don't. You may have a more sensitive stomach than I do, though.

My advice is to do your own research and decide what risks you are willing to take. This applies not just in China but in all developing countries, including all the ones discussed in this book.

A Few More Words You Should Know

Do I Really Have to Learn to Speak Chinese?

In most countries where you don't speak the language, a translation app or phrasebook such as the Vegan Passport produced by The Vegan Society is enough to communicate your needs.

China is a special case, though, so it's a good idea to learn how to pronounce a few key phrases. The biggest challenge by far for travelers in China (both vegan and non-vegan) is overcoming the language barrier.

If you stick to the well-trodden tourist trail, which includes destinations such as Beijing, Shanghai, Xian, Hong Kong and Yangshuo, then you are more likely to come across staff in restaurants and hotels who speak at least a little English. If you venture off this beaten path, however, you will soon find yourself struggling to communicate if you don't have a few key Chinese words and phrases under your belt.

All Chinese words given below and throughout this chapter are written in both pinyin (a system for writing Chinese using the Latin alphabet) and in simplified Chinese characters (the type of characters used throughout mainland China).

If you just want to show the word or phrase to a Chinese person, show them the simplified characters. If you want to try pronouncing it yourself, however, I strongly advise that you learn a bit about how to read pinyin and how to correctly pronounce the tones and other sounds used in Chinese.

During my early travels in China, I very quickly realized the importance of learning to say at least a few words in Chinese. Even though I'd managed to get along just fine when traveling in many other countries where I didn't speak the language, in China I felt like I was constantly running up against a brick wall called "the language barrier".

Anywhere else in the world, if I walked into a hotel lobby, the staff there would figure out pretty quickly what I was looking for, and they would show me a room. In China, that wasn't how it worked.

Instead, I would be hit with a barrage of Chinese that was completely incomprehensible to me. I couldn't just pay for a room and be done with it. There was always lots of paperwork to be filled out, and if I didn't understand exactly which documents were needed, I was pretty much stuck.

I met with similar frustrations when attempting to buy train tickets, or order a meal in a restaurant, or do any of the other daily tasks that should have been simple but were anything but.

And so, reluctantly at first, I downloaded some beginner level language learning podcasts from a site called ChinesePod and began studying Chinese. I say "reluctantly" because I was in the middle of learning Russian at the time, and I really didn't want to confuse myself by adding yet another new language.

Chinese held little appeal for me, probably because I associated it with frustration and difficulty. I viewed my study of it purely as a survival skill, and I just wanted to learn the bare minimum that would enable me to put food in my belly and a roof over my head at night.

And then, something completely unexpected happened: I got hooked.

Suddenly those loud, abrasive sounds turned into actual words. Words that I could use to communicate and be understood! I became fascinated by the tonal structure of the language and the complex characters used to write it.

After a few months, I dropped my Russian studies altogether and began devoting huge chunks of my free time to learning more and more Chinese. After a few years of study, I was able to pass the highest level of the standardized Chinese proficiency exam (HSK 6), and I began translating documents from Chinese into English for the United Nations.

Now, it's obviously not necessary for you to master the Chinese language to that degree. However, I do highly recommend learning at least a few key words and phrases if you're heading to China. You'll be surprised at how much easier life in China is with a few words under your belt.

And, if you're anything like me, the success you have with those first few words will encourage you to keep learning more, and who knows where that may lead. Learning a language that's so completely different from your own is a lot of fun, and it really opens a window onto a whole new culture and worldview.

But even if you just stick to a few dozen words, your experience in China will be vastly improved. Unfortunately, many people who attempt to learn Chinese get frustrated with the pronunciation and give up straight away.

Chinese is a tonal language, which means that the same word pronounced in four different tones of voice can have four completely different meanings. You can imagine, then, how important it is to get the pronunciation right.

Luckily, the folks at ChinesePod.com have put together a fantastic Chinese pronunciation course. If you're heading to China, do yourself a favor and check out their Say It Right course.

Key Words and Phrases

In Chinese, there is no obvious, well-understood word for "vegan" that would differentiate veganism from lacto-ovo vegetarianism. When explaining your diet, it's best to start with the phrase "wǒ chī sù" (我吃素).

This is the most widely understood way of saying that you eat plants and not animal-based foods. It may very well be interpreted as meaning "vegan" right from the start. Dairy products are barely used in China anyway, so that's pretty much a non-issue. The only further clarification you'll need to give is that you don't eat eggs.

English	Simplified Chinese	Pinyin
I'm a vegetarian/vegan	我吃素	wǒ chī sù
I don't eat any type of meat.	我不吃任何肉类	wǒ bù chī rènhé ròulèi
I don't eat fish.	我不吃鱼	wǒ bù chī yú
I don't eat eggs.	我不吃鸡蛋	wǒ bù chī jīdàn
Does this have meat in it?	这个有肉吗？	zhège yǒu ròu ma?
Can you make it without meat?	可以做没有肉的吗？	kéyǐ zuò méiyǒu ròu de ma?
Can you replace the meat with tofu?	可以用豆腐代替肉吗？	kéyǐ yòng dòufu dàitì ròu ma?
Thank you!	谢谢！	xièxie!
It's delicious!	很好吃！	hěn hǎo chī!

Vegan Food in Chinese Restaurants outside China

Many of the Chinese immigrants who have opened Chinese restaurants in other countries around the world hail from Hong Kong or the neighboring southern province of Guangdong. For this reason, most Chinese restaurants outside China serve a variant of southern Chinese cooking that has been adapted to the tastes of the country where the restaurant is located.

If you're eating at a Chinese restaurant in the US or another Western country, the menu will probably be divided into the sections typically found in Western menus: appetizers, main dishes, side dishes, desserts, etc.

In the appetizer section, you will almost always find vegetable spring rolls (素春卷), and perhaps also vegetable-filled dumplings (素菜饺). The vegetable spring rolls sometimes contain eggs, but you can often find them without.

The main dishes section of the menu is often subdivided by the type of meat in the dish. There are generally long lists of dishes made with chicken, beef, pork, etc., and often a much shorter "vegetables" section.

But don't dismiss those meaty sections of the menu just yet! Any Chinese restaurant worth its salt will have tofu on hand, so you can ask to replace any of those meats with tofu, or perhaps eggplant or mushrooms.

For example, if you see "sweet and sour pork" (咕咾肉), "Sichuan beef" (四川牛肉) or "kung pao chicken" (宫保鸡丁) on the menu, you can ask for "sweet and sour tofu" (咕咾豆腐), "Sichuan tofu" (四川豆腐) or "kung pao tofu" (宫保豆腐) instead. Some restaurants will even have mock meats, which are made from either seitan (wheat gluten), soy, or sometimes konjac.

Now, about that "vegetables" section of the menu. If it's labeled "vegetables" and not "vegetarian", then be aware that some of the dishes may still contain small amounts of meat, even though the main ingredients are plant-based.

Tofu, for example, is an important ingredient in Chinese cuisine in its own right and is not viewed as a meat substitute like it is in the West. This means that a dish featuring tofu may also contain meat, though you can ask for it without. For example, mapo tofu (麻婆豆腐) usually contains minced beef.

There are sure to be some naturally vegan dishes in this section, though, such as broccoli with garlic sauce （蒜蓉西兰花） or a simple dish of mixed Chinese vegetables.

In addition to the "vegetables" section, there may also be a separate rice and noodle section of the menu with options like chow mein, which is stir-fried noodles (炒面). The wheat noodles served in restaurants sometimes contain egg, but they will also have rice noodles available, and these are always vegan. Just ask for the noodles to be tossed only with vegetables and not with fried egg.

Dairy products are very rarely used in Chinese cuisine, so the dessert menu is likely to include vegan options such as banana fritters or sweetened sticky rice balls.

Extra Resources

ChinesePod. Learning at least a few key phrases in Chinese will really go a loooong way when trying to order food and communicate your needs, and self-study with podcasts and videos is a great way to learn.

With ChinesePod's Say It Right video pronunciation course, you'll have the skills and confidence to express yourself in Chinese and actually be understood. The first few lessons are free, or you can gain access to the whole course and much more when you sign up for an annual premium subscription. They're even offering Veggie Planet readers $50 off! Just use the promo code: VEGANPOD.

The Chinese Vegan Kitchen. For some easy but authentic vegan Chinese recipes you can prepare in your own kitchen, check out this book by Donna Klein. It includes more than 225 vegan recipes.

China Sichuan Food is a recipe blog written by Elaine Luo, who grew up in Sichuan and now lives elsewhere in China. Despite the name, her blog includes recipe from other regions of China besides Sichuan. Not all recipes are vegan, but the ones that are are tagged for easy identification.

The China Study. To learn more about the plant-based diet traditionally eaten in China and its nutritional and health implications, there is no better source than this seminal work by T. Colin Campbell, Ph.D. It explains in layman's terms the results of the most comprehensive nutrition study ever conducted.

The Hutong is a culture exchange center in Beijing that offers a vast range of culinary activities, including culinary market tours and cooking classes. Many of the classes are veggie-friendly, with topics like making your own tofu or cooking with seasonal vegetables, and The Hutong can offer a private, completely veganized version of one of their other cooking classes on request.

China Vegans, China: Vegan, Eco friendly, Spiritual Events, Places, and *Vegetarian China* are three different Facebook groups that you could join to connect with vegans in China. This is a great way to get local insider tips and maybe make some new friends.

Chapter Three

Ethiopian Cuisine

Vegan Food in Ethiopia

Even though Ethiopians do seem to have a great love for meat, the cuisine of Ethiopia (and neighboring Eritrea) is full of naturally vegan dishes. This is largely because of the fasting tradition in the Ethiopian Orthodox Church.

Many religious people fast every Wednesday and Friday, as well as during Lent, in the days leading up to Christmas, and at other fasting periods. Fasting doesn't mean that they don't eat at all; it just means they eat vegan.

If you're planning a trip to Ethiopia or Eritrea, you might want to consider timing your visit to coincide with one of the fasting periods. The largest are the Hudade Tsome, which runs for the 55 days leading up to Ethiopian Easter, and the Tsome Neviyat, which runs for 43 days before Ethiopian Christmas.

There is also a 16-day fast in August to celebrate the assumption of the Virgin Mary. Check the dates for Ethiopian religious holidays, as they are different from the dates observed by Catholic and Protestant churches. Christmas is celebrated on January 7th, for example. Easter is a moveable feast day but often falls a bit later in Ethiopia than in the West. There is an Ethiopian nun who maintains an updated list of fasting days on Facebook (see thenomadicvegan.com/resources for the link).

Outside of these periods, fasting food is still pretty readily available, except during the holidays right *after* these fasting periods, e.g. Easter and Christmas. At these times of the year, the locals will be making up for lost time and digging into their favorite meaty dishes, so fasting foods will be harder to come by.

So, once you decide on the dates of your trip to Ethiopia, what will you eat when you get there? Ethiopian and Eritrean cuisine is unlike any other world cuisine. If you've never tasted it before, you're in for a real treat!

The first thing to know is that the food is eaten not with a knife and fork but with the hands. You will rarely see cutlery on an Ethiopian table. Actually, when I say that Ethiopian food is eaten with the hands, what I really mean is that it's eaten with just the right hand. It's bad manners to use the left hand for eating, as it's reserved for other things like wiping your bottom after going to the bathroom.

Eating with your hand might sound messy, but it's easy when you have a big piece of *injera* (sourdough bread) that you can use to mop up the stews and vegetables on your plate. No Ethiopian meal is complete without *injera*. We'll talk more about this essential staple in the next section.

In addition to *injera*, you will also see the word *wot* quite often on an Ethiopian menu. It means "stew" or "sauce", and Ethiopian cuisine includes a huge variety of them. Typically, small portions of several different *wot* and other dishes are served together on top of fresh *injera*. The many different *wot* can generally be divided into two types.

First, there are the *kay wot*, which, thanks to the *berbere* spice mix added to them, are red in color and spicy in flavor. *Berbere* is a spice blend made with red chili peppers and other spices like ginger, cloves, and cinnamon. It is a key component of many Ethiopian dishes. *Mitmita* is the spiciest type of *berbere* because it contains the seeds of the chili pepper, whereas in the milder *awaze* the seeds are left out.

If you don't like spicy food, then you'll probably want to avoid *kay wot* and instead stick to *alicha wot*, which are much milder. These are often referred to as "Ethiopian curries" because they are seasoned with turmeric, which gives them a golden hue. In addition to the turmeric, *alicha wot* also contain garlic, ginger, and green chili peppers, so they do still have a bit of a kick to them.

The best way to sample a variety of vegan dishes is by ordering a *yetsom beyaynetu*. This is a purely vegan combination platter that will allow you to taste a little bit of everything. Almost every Ethiopian restaurant abroad will have *yetsom beyaynetu* as a standard menu item. In Ethiopia itself, restaurants will always offer these platters on Wednesdays and Fridays (when the locals are fasting), and some will offer them every day of the week.

The *yetsom beyaynetu* is often described on English menus as a "vegetarian platter", but in reality, it's not just vegetarian but also vegan. It's worth pointing out that, outside Western countries, many cultures don't make a distinction between vegetarian and vegan.

This is especially true of cultures whose cuisines do not often use dairy products, which includes many of the cuisines described in this book. Westerners often think that, while vegetarian options might be relatively easy to find when eating out, vegan options are much fewer and farther between. The reality is, though, that in many ethnic restaurants almost all the vegetarian options will also be vegan. This is certainly true in Ethiopian restaurants.

Vegan or Veganizable Dishes to Seek Out

Injera – እንጀራ a spongy, unleavened, sourdough bread that doubles as both plate and cutlery. Ethiopian meals are typically served on a large, round piece of *injera*. Small servings of various stews and other dishes are then placed on top of the *injera*, and a second piece of *injera* is used to scoop up the stews and bring them to the mouth.

Injera is traditionally made from teff - a gluten-free grain that grows in abundance in Ethiopia. This makes Ethiopian food a great choice for celiacs and people with gluten intolerance as well as vegans.

Yetsom beyaynetu - የፆም በያይነቱ - a vegan sampling platter of many different legume-based stews and vegetable dishes served on top of *injera*. Most commonly, *shiro* (see description below) is ladled onto the center of the *injera* and other dishes are placed around the edges. Ordering a *yetsom beyaynetu* is a fantastic way to sample a variety of the many vegan dishes that Ethiopian cuisine has to offer. If you don't know what to order, start with this.

Shiro - ሽሮ/ተጋቢኖ - a very popular dish made from finely ground chickpeas cooked in the spicy red *berbere* spice blend that flavors so many of the dishes in this cuisine. In addition to chickpeas, *shiro* is sometimes also made with lentils and broad beans. There are multiple types of *shiro*, ranging in texture from the soupy, thin *shiro wot* to the much thicker *shiro tegamino*.

Misir wot - የምስር ወጥ - the word "*misir*" means "lentils", so *misir wot* is a stew made from split red lentils that are simmered in a sauce flavored with spicy *berbere*. It's a very common dish that often appears on a *yetsom beyaynetu*. There are a number of possible additions that can be made to this basic dish to create different variations, such as tomato, tomato and sliced okra, or sautéed mushrooms.

Atakilt alicha - አልጫ አታክልት - since "*atakilt*" simply means "vegetables" in Amharic (the official language of Ethiopia), there are many possible variations of this mild vegetable stew. The most common is a combination of cabbage, carrots, and potatoes simmered in a light sauce. This is what you'll usually find in restaurants. Other vegetables that are sometimes included are cauliflower, onions, and green beans.

Fasolia be'karot - ፎሶሊያ በካሮት - *fasolia* are green beans (sometimes also called French beans or string beans), and can you guess what "*karot*" means? If you guessed "carrot", then you're getting the hang of this. The names of Ethiopian dishes might sound complicated, but they are often quite simple once you break them down into individual words. In this dish, green beans are braised with carrots and caramelized onions in a garlicky onion sauce.

Kay sir dinich - ቀይስር እና ድንች - Here's another example of a dish whose name is self-explanatory once you learn a few words of Amharic. "*Kay sir*" literally means "red root", and it is the Amharic name for beets. "*Dinich*", on the other hand, is the word for "potatoes". This dish, then, is a mix of beets and potatoes. At first glance, you might not see the potatoes, because the juice from the beets turns the whole dish a deep purple color. *Kay sir dinich* is usually a mild *alicha*, but it could also be made as a *wot*. In either case, it adds beautiful color to a *yetsom beyaynetu*.

Gomen - ጎመን - the word "*gomen*" generally refers to collard greens, which is the most common type of dark, leafy green vegetable eaten in Ethiopia. Other types of greens could also be used in this dish, though, such as kale, chard or even beet greens. The greens are chopped very finely and stewed until tender. This is another dish that almost always features in a *yetsom beyaynetu,* and it adds both nutrition and color to the meal.

Firfir - ፍርፍር - is a warm dish made of small pieces of shredded *injera* that are mixed with lots of sauce from a *kay wot* or *alicha wot*. The *injera* and *wot* sauce are stir-fried together so that the bread absorbs the sauce and softens. It is

65

typically eaten for breakfast as a way to use up the leftover *injera* and *wot* from the previous day. Sometimes *firfir* is made with crusty bread instead of *injera*.

Fitfit - ፍትፍት - is similar to *firfir*, except that it's served cold or at room temperature, whereas *firfir* is served warm. The sauce can be made from any number of ingredients, but it usually doesn't contain any *berbere*, whereas *firfir* does. It can perhaps best be described as an *injera* salad. There are many different variations of both *firfir* and *fitfit*, depending on the type of sauce used.

Vegan Food in Ethiopian Restaurants outside Ethiopia

The Ethiopian food served outside of Ethiopia is usually pretty authentic, and you are sure to find many of the dishes described in this chapter. In fact, in some ways, eating vegan in Ethiopian restaurants outside the country is easier than in Ethiopia itself, because you don't have to worry about keeping track of the day of the week or the many fasting periods.

Outside the country, restaurants offer a *yetsom beyaynetu* year round, and this is probably what you will want to order. Sure, they will most likely have dishes like *shiro*, *misir wot*

Veggie Planet

and *atakilt alicha* available to order à la carte, but why not just get a big platter and enjoy a bit of everything?

Keep in mind that there's no standardized way of transliterating Amharic into English. This means that some of the dishes described in this book may be spelled differently on menus. Even if you don't recognize the name right away, though, the menu will normally include a description of each dish.

In cities with large Eritrean communities, you are more likely to find an Eritrean restaurant than an Ethiopian one. This is certainly true in Geneva, Switzerland, for example, where I lived for about six years. My favorite restaurant in town was a little hole-in-the-wall place behind the train station, called Red Sea Restaurant, that's run by an Eritrean family. It's nothing fancy, but I loved it for the warm welcome, the cheap prices, and of course the food!

They offer an all-you-can-eat buffet on Saturday evenings, and on the weekends when I was in town I would always try to make it there for dinner. It wasn't until after I became vegan that I realized that more than half of the buffet dishes were vegan! I still make a point of going back there whenever I'm in Geneva. Sadly, my current city of Lisbon doesn't have any Ethiopian or Eritrean restaurants, and it's something I really miss.

I mention this to let you know that, if you can't find any listings for Ethiopian restaurants in your area, you should try looking for Eritrean restaurants instead. The cuisine is largely the same; they just might have different names for some of the dishes.

Another thing to keep in mind in restaurants outside of Ethiopia and Eritrea is that the *injera* is not always made with pure teff flour.

This is because teff can be hard to come by outside these two countries, and even when available it's very expensive. So, even when teff is used, it's often mixed with other types of flour.

The *injera* will still be vegan no matter what type of flour it's made with, but if you follow a gluten-free diet you should be aware that *injera* made with grains other than teff is often not gluten free. With the growing popularity of gluten-free diets, however, some restaurants are offering to make pure teff *injera* for an extra charge with advance notice.

Extra Resources

Teff Love: Adventures in Vegan Ethiopian Cooking by Kittee Berns. The idea of preparing Ethiopian dishes yourself can certainly seem daunting. There are so many unfamiliar spices and powders, and *injera* takes three days to ferment! But if you're feeling up to the challenge, Kittee Berns is the one to teach you how to do it. Even if you don't end up making any of the recipes in her book, it's a great source of information about this fascinating cuisine, and the photos are mouthwatering.

Mesob Across America: Ethiopian Food in the U.S.A. is a book written by Harry Kloman, an American journalist and teacher at the University of Pittsburgh who has become quite an authority on Ethiopian cuisine and culture. In this book, Kloman takes an in-depth look at the cuisine's history and culture and also explores the history of how Ethiopian restaurants emerged in the United States.

Kloman also keeps a blog on Ethiopian food, where he shares a wealth of information about the cuisine as well as listings of Ethiopian restaurants all across the United States.

Emahoy Hannah's Facebook page is helpful for finding out the dates of the various fasting periods. She is an Ethiopian nun who lives in a monastery in southern Florida, and each year she makes an updated post with all of the fasting dates for that year.

There are a couple of Facebook groups for vegans in Addis Ababa, but they don't have many members. Rather than joining these groups, you're better off contacting the folks who run the *Vegan Ethiopia Facebook page* to see if they can answer your questions and/or put you in touch with the local vegan community.

Chapter Four

Greek Cuisine

Vegan Food in Greece

Greece is not widely known for its vegetarian and vegan dishes. In fact, when I tell people how vegan-friendly Greece really is, they are always surprised. Most people, when they think of Greek food, think of a *gyro* (a sandwich stuffed with meat cooked on a vertical spit like a Turkish döner kebab), or perhaps *souvlaki* (chunks of meat grilled on a skewer).

It's true that both these meat dishes *are* commonly found in Greece, and perhaps and even more so in Greek restaurants outside Greece. But traditional Greek cuisine has so much more to offer!

I discovered this first-hand when I visited Greece in 2014. I had been transitioning towards a vegan lifestyle for a few months, and I really wanted to be completely vegan, but I was scared.

Scared that being vegan was going to ruin travel. That sounds ridiculous to me now, but at the time I really believed it. I decided to face my fears by taking vegan travel out for a test drive. I would attempt to stay vegan for the duration of my three weeks in Greece. If it turned out that it was possible after all, then I would have to reevaluate my assumptions.

Not only was vegan travel in Greece possible, it was an absolute joy! I was completely blown away by the huge number of naturally vegan dishes that appeared on virtually every menu in every restaurant across the country. Needless to say, I remained vegan for the duration of the trip and never looked back.

I'm not the only visitor who's been surprised at the abundance of vegan food in Greece. Caitlin Galer-Unti, who blogs at The Vegan Word, had a similar experience there:

"I chose Santorini after a trip to the hairdresser earlier this year where she reignited a long-lost desire to go there (fueled by countless photos of white houses, blue-domed church roofs, and mile upon mile of endless sea, stretching out towards the horizon and meeting the sky in a fuzzy blue line). She also regaled me with tales of vegan food and friendly Santorinians who were always willing to make something vegan for you (yes, my hairdresser is vegan too!).

In fact, Santorini was even more beautiful than the pictures and much more vegan-friendly than I'd anticipated even after many people had told me I wouldn't have a problem finding vegan stuff there. I wasn't quite prepared to be able to go into just about any restaurant and order a vegan meal.

This is helped by the fact that food is usually cooked in olive oil (not butter), so you can order a lot of vegetable side dishes, and pretty much all restaurants have fava (a hummus-like puree of split peas) and Greek salad (tomato, cucumbers, and olives, sometimes with the addition of pepper and capers – just ask them to hold the cheese, which is not a problem since they usually add it at the end)."

The reason why Greece is such a vegan-friendly destination is largely because, like Ethiopia and Eritrea, Greece also has a strong fasting tradition. Indeed, most Orthodox Christian countries do. Practicing Orthodox Christians in Greece are encouraged to fast every Wednesday and Friday, and also during specific fasting periods throughout the year. Sound familiar?

Some of these fasting periods last for several weeks, such as the ones leading up to Easter and Christmas. In total, there are more than 180 fasting days in the Greek Orthodox calendar!

Like in Ethiopia and Eritrea, fasting in Greece doesn't mean not eating at all. It just means following certain dietary restrictions. And, luckily for vegans, those dietary restrictions consist of eliminating almost all animal products from the diet.

The only exceptions to this ban on animal products are honey and certain species of aquatic animals. On fasting days, Greeks will not eat fish, but they will eat shrimp, squid and other invertebrate animals who live in the sea.

With this caveat in mind, the easiest way to order a vegan meal in Greece is to ask for a *nistisimo* (νηστίσιμο) dish, as *nistisimo* is the Greek word for fasting food.

This is a handy shortcut because, despite the huge number of naturally vegan dishes in Greek cuisine, the concept of veganism itself is not widely known or understood. If you try asking your waiter which dishes on the menu are vegan, you will probably get a blank stare.

The menu is bound to be full of vegan dishes, mind you, but you could easily miss out on tasting them just because of miscommunication. You'll have much better luck if you rely on the locally familiar concept of fasting to get your point across.

Just remember that your waiter might then suggest some seafood dishes, so it's best to specify that you don't eat those either.

Once you've made it clear what you do and don't eat, you can start choosing from among the many different options. You may find that you don't even make it past the appetizer section of the menu!

Some of the best vegan specialties in Greek cuisine are *mezedhes* (μεζέδες, or *meze* (μεζές) in the singular form). These are dips and other dishes served in small portions, often accompanied by *rakι* or some other alcoholic drink.

Mezedhes can be served as a prelude to a main course, but it's also perfectly acceptable to order several of these dishes and call it a meal. Locals do it all the time. Sometimes restaurants will offer a *meze* platter, but if not, you can always just order them à la carte.

Of course, there are also a number of vegan main dishes in Greek cuisine. Below are just a few examples of the types of offerings you can expect to find.

Vegan or Veganizable Dishes to Seek Out

Skordalia- Σκορδαλιά - basically a very garlicky mashed potato dish. It can be used as a dip with bread or served as an accompaniment to a main dish. Garlic is added raw, not cooked, so the garlic flavor can be quite strong. In addition to the mashed potato version, another variation involves replacing the potatoes with stale bread, which is sometimes mixed with crushed walnuts or almonds.

Dolmadhes- Ντολμάδες - grape vine leaves that have been rolled up into a cigar shape, stuffed with a mix of rice, herbs, and spices, and then boiled. While you can often find them canned in supermarkets, the fresh ones available in restaurants are usually far superior. There is also a version made with meat, so be sure to ask for the meatless one. Even then, the meatless one is often served with yogurt on the side, so make it clear that you don't want that.

Tomatokeftedes - Ντοματοκεφτέδες - fritters made with tomato and mint, shaped into small patties, and fried in olive oil. You might also come across other fritters in Greece made with different vegetables, such as *melitzanokeftedes* made with eggplant or *kolokithokeftedes* made with zucchini. In my experience, though, the *tomatokeftedes* are the ones most likely to be vegan, as the others often have eggs or grated cheese added to them.

Melitzanosalata - Μελιτζανοσαλάτα - a cold dip made with roasted eggplant, lemon juice, olive oil, and herbs and spices. It's served as a *meze* with bread and is similar to the *baba ghanoush* found in the Middle East. Some places do add mayonnaise or yogurt to their *melitzanosalata*, so check to be sure. One particular version of *melitzanosalata* is known as

"Constantinople style" or *politiki melitzanosalata* and is notable for its chunky texture. It's considered to be a salad (note the word *"salata"* in the name) rather than a sauce or spread.

Briám- **Μπριάμ** - an oven-baked dish of mixed vegetables similar to the *ratatouille* found in southern France. The vegetables used can vary, but they always include potatoes and zucchini, and you'll usually find tomatoes and eggplant in there too.

Gigantes- **Γίγαντες** - as their name suggests, *gigantes* are large (some might even say giant!) white beans cooked in a typical Mediterranean sauce of tomatoes, onions, and herbs. In English, these beans are known as lima beans, or sometimes butter beans, but there is no butter in the dish. *Gigantes* can be served either as a *meze* or as a main dish.

Gemista- **Γεμιστά** - this dish is made by stuffing a mixture of rice and herbs into either tomatoes or red bell peppers and then roasting them in the oven. Sometimes it can even be a mix of tomatoes *and* bell peppers. It's usually served with thick French fries, which are themselves a delicacy not to be missed in Greece. The stuffing mixture occasionally contains minced meat, but usually it's made vegan.

Aginares a la Polita - Αγκινάρες αλά πολίτα - a stew made with artichokes, carrots, and potatoes and flavored with lemon and dill. If you're an artichoke fan like I am, another similar dish worth seeking out is *arakas me aginares*, which is a stew made with artichokes and peas.

Spanakopita - Σπανακόπιτα - a pie made from a flaky pastry dough and filled with spinach. Savory pies are sold on every street corner in Greece and are the quintessential Greek fast food. Most versions contain some kind of cheese, but *spanakopita*, at least in its *nistisimo* version, is filled only with spinach.

This is a delicious way to get your dark leafy greens while traveling! If you see *hortapita*, this is essentially the same thing, except that it might contain different leafy greens instead of spinach. Sometimes bakeries will put a *nistisimo* label in the display case to mark their *nistisimo* pies and other items, but if not you can always ask.

Soutzouki - Σουτζούκι - these log-shaped sweets are made by threading walnuts or other nuts onto a string, dipping them several times into grape must, and then leaving the whole thing out to dry for several days. Be careful if you ask for this by name without seeing it, as the word "*soutzouki*" also refers to a sausage made from meat. In fact, this dessert is named after the sausage because it has a similar shape. In Cyprus, the same dessert is known as *soutzoukos*.

Disclaimer: While all these dishes are usually vegan, recipes do vary, so ask if they are *nistisimo* to be sure. *Nistisimo* is your magic word in Greece. If you only learn one word of Greek, make it this one.

Vegan Food in Greek Restaurants outside Greece

Greek eateries outside Greece typically fall into one of two categories. First, you have the gyro sandwich stand, which is pretty much indistinguishable from the (Turkish) döner kebab stand or the (Middle Eastern) shawarma stand.

The culinary traditions of Greece, Turkey, and the Middle East have mixed with each other over many centuries, with each one influencing the others. Many of the dishes described in this chapter are found not only in Greece, but also in Turkey, and to a lesser extent in other countries of the Middle East. Of course, recipes are often changed and adapted as they pass from one region to the next.

People from outside these regions have understandably become a bit confused about these culinary traditions, and some dishes that we *think* are from Greece are actually from the Middle East.

A prime example of this is the fried balls of ground chickpeas known as falafel. Popular throughout the Middle East, falafel is a deep-fried ball that is usually made from ground chickpeas, though it can also be made from ground fava beans, or a combination of the two.

Now, exactly *which* Middle Eastern country can lay claim to the invention of falafel is a whole other hotly debated topic, but it's safe to say that falafel was created in the Arab Levant, *not* in Greece.

Nevertheless, gyro stands outside Greece almost always offer a falafel sandwich in addition to their meat-based sandwiches. Perhaps this is because their customers have come to expect falafel from the very similar-looking sandwich stands run by their Arab counterparts, and so the gyro stands want to be able to compete on an equal footing.

Whatever the reason, it's a welcome adaptation for vegetarians and vegans. A falafel wrap from one of these ubiquitous stands is a cheap, convenient and reliable vegan option that has become the fall-back meal for many vegans whenever they find themselves in not-so-vegan-friendly locations.

The second category of Greek eatery found outside of Greece is the "typical" Greek restaurant. These can sometimes be a bit kitsch, with tables and chairs painted in blue and white (the colors of the Greek flag) and perhaps even a show involving traditional Greek dancing and some plate smashing.

The menu is likely to emphasize the meat-based dishes of Greek cuisine, but you should still be able to find a few vegan options. Just watch out for embellishments aimed at pleasing foreign palates, such as adding cheddar cheese to *gemista* or other dishes that would normally be vegan.

Even if there aren't any suitable main dishes, you should still be able to put together a meal of *mezedhes* such as *dolmadhes* or *gigantes*. Restaurants like these will probably also have *hummus* - the chickpea and tahini dip that is a perennial favorite with vegans and non-vegans alike.

Many visitors to Greece are shocked to find out that *hummus* is not a Greek dish and is not widely available in the country. In Greek restaurants outside Greece, however, it's almost always on the menu, which of course just perpetuates the confusion. Another menu item you're guaranteed to find is Greek salad, so at the very least you can always order one of these without the feta cheese.

Extra Resources

The Greek Vegan. If you'd like to cook some of these delicious dishes yourself, the Greek Vegan website is a good place to go for recipes. Kiki Vagianos, who runs the site, also produces Nisteia Magazine, which features authentic, traditional Greek vegan recipes.

Yasou: A Magical Fusion of Greek & Middle Eastern Vegan Cuisine. This recipe book by Miriam Sorrell offers a glimpse into the potpourri of flavors created by fusing Greek with Turkish and Middle Eastern cuisine. Sorrell grew up in Malta and was born to a Greek Cypriot father and a mother with Greek, Turkish, and Maltese origins.

Bamboo Vegan is an all-vegan shop in the center of Athens that sells a wide range of vegan cooking ingredients and packaged, ready-to-eat foods. You can find Violife cheese here, which is a delicious Greek brand of vegan cheese that's great for melting on pizza. Bamboo also sells fresh baked goods, like muffins, cupcakes, and savory cheese pies. In addition to the brick-and-mortar shop in Athens, they also run an online shop that will ship anywhere in Greece.

Vegan Life Festival. On 5 November 2016, Greece held its very first vegan festival. This is a clear sign that the vegan movement is growing in the country, so maybe in the future veganism will be widely understood and the magic word "*nistisimo*" won't be so necessary. The festival website is only in Greek, but you can contact them through their Facebook page to find out about upcoming events.

Vegans in Greece, *Vegetarians and Vegans of Greece*, and *vegans in greece* are three of the Facebook groups where you could connect with local vegans before traveling to Greece.

Chapter Five

Turkish Cuisine

Vegan Food in Turkey

While restaurants in Turkey tend to tout their meat-heavy dishes to foreign tourists, if you can look past all the kebab you will find that there are many local specialties for vegans to enjoy. The more authentic, home-cooked dishes focus not on meat but on beans and vegetables and are usually cooked in olive oil rather than animal-based fats. Legumes, and lentils in particular, are one of the foundations of the Turkish diet.

A great place to try these plant-based dishes is at *ev yemekleri*. The name literally means "home cooking" restaurants, and these family-run establishments serve authentic Turkish food at reasonable prices.

The many vegan meze dishes are another great option and are widely available. Meze are appetizers that are often served before a main course. They are most commonly found in the traditional bars or restaurants known as *meyhane*.

Another good place to look for a vegan meal of meze is, oddly enough, Turkey's many seafood restaurants. The tradition in these restaurants is to first bring out a plate of cold meze, many of which will be vegan. Then comes a round of hot meze, and only after that is fish served. But it's perfectly acceptable to eat just the meze and forego the fish course.

You will find an abundance of vegan options among the meze dishes, so it's easy to create a full meal by combining a few meze with some delicious Turkish bread to soak it all up.

Street food is a huge part of Turkish culture, and quite a few of the most common street food snacks are vegan or can be made vegan on request. These foods are cheap and filling, and the stalls that sell them are a great place to rub elbows with the locals and really immerse yourself in Turkish culture.

One vegan street food that you probably *won't* find in Turkey, however, is falafel. Nope, contrary to what your local kebab shop has led you to believe, falafel is not Turkish! In fact, most Turks have never heard of it.

Hummus is not strictly Turkish either, but it is sometimes eaten in Turkey, particularly in the eastern part of the country. In other regions, it's less common. But don't worry!

You'll be so busy making new discoveries in this rich and varied cuisine that you won't miss that falafel wrap one bit. Here are just a few dishes to get you started.

Vegan or Veganizable Dishes to Seek Out

Kahvaltı tabağı (breakfast plate) - the typical breakfast plate includes tea, fruit juice, cucumbers, tomatoes, olives, bread, jams, and other spreads such as *tahini pekmez* (tahini and grape molasses mixed together). It will also include other non-vegan items like eggs, cheese, and butter, but you can ask to leave these off. You might also find breakfast plates that include *gözleme* or *acılı ezme* (see below for descriptions of these dishes).

The Turkish word *kahvaltı* can actually mean either "breakfast" or "a snack or light refreshment", so *kahvaltı* plates are often served throughout the day. This suits me perfectly, since I rarely eat anything before noon, but at the same time I absolutely love breakfast foods. I've even been known to eat a bowl of oatmeal for both lunch and dinner.

Çiğ köfte - a popular and inexpensive street food sold at many stalls throughout the country. The word "*çiğ*" means "raw", and traditionally this dish was in fact made from raw meat. Gross. Under modern health regulations, however, this is no longer allowed. The modified version of *çiğ köfte* that is sold today is a spread made from bulgur wheat, ground walnuts, tomatoes and red pepper paste.

It's often spicy, and you have the option of topping it with an additional spicy sauce as well, and/or sweet pomegranate syrup. You can also choose whether you'd like it served in a wrap (called a "*dürüm*") or on a plate over a bed of lettuce. In addition to the take-away stands that serve nothing but *çiğ köfte*, it's also sometimes served as a meze in restaurants.

Gözleme - often translated as "pancake" in English, *gözleme* are actually nothing like the sweet, fluffy pancakes that are eaten with maple syrup in North America. Instead, they are made from a hand-rolled dough that contains no milk or eggs, or even sugar for that matter. They are perhaps more like French *crêpes* than American pancakes, but most versions are savory, not sweet.

The most common vegan fillings for *gözleme* are spinach and/or potato. Some places will also offer mushrooms, onions, and parsley. Just ask for yours *peynirsiz* ("without cheese") to be sure that there's no cheese mixed in with the filling. Note that some places may use butter to grease the pan, while others will use olive or sunflower oil.

Kumpir - a baked potato piled high with any and every kind of topping you can imagine. You get to choose the toppings, so just stick to the vegan ones like olives, sweet corn, peas, pickled vegetables, hot chili sauce, mushrooms, cucumbers, jalapeño peppers, etc. Normally, before adding the toppings they will mash some butter and cheese into the potato, so make it clear from the beginning that you don't want that.

These stuffed baked potatoes can be found all over Turkey, but Istanbul's Ortaköy neighborhood is particularly famous for them. There's even a street there known as "Kumpir Sokak" (Baked Potato Street).

İmam Bayıldı - the name literally means "the imam fainted". This is a popular dish consisting of an eggplant that is stuffed with a mix of tomatoes, onions and garlic and roasted until it's incredibly soft. It can be served as either a meze or as a main dish.

Güveç - much like the word "casserole" in English, the word "*güveç*" is used to designate both a traditional clay pot and any dish cooked in such a pot in the oven. Recipes vary widely, but you can often find vegan *güveç* made with eggplant, zucchini, and other vegetables.

Mercimek köftesi - this is a plant-based version of the grilled lamb meatballs that are so common in Turkey. These are completely meat free and are made from red lentils and bulgur wheat. *Mercimek köftesi* are typically served at room temperature on a bed of lettuce.

Zeytinyağlı - this is a broad term used for any number of vegetable dishes cooked in olive oil, which are typically eaten cold as a meze. Turkish cuisine includes a wide variety of such dishes, and they are usually vegan.

Zeytinyağlı enginar, for example, is an artichoke heart filled with peas, potato, and carrots. Other examples of *zeytinyağlı* include *zeytinyağlı pırasa* (leeks, carrots, and rice in olive oil) and zeytinyağlı taze fasulye (green beans in garlic, tomatoes and olive oil).

Sarma - this is actually a subcategory of *zeytinyağlı* dishes. *Sarma* can be made from various types of leafy greens (usually grape vine leaves, cabbage, chard or cherry leaves). These are filled with a mixture of rice, herbs, and spices, cooked in olive oil and rolled into cigar shapes.

They are then eaten cold. Note that there is another type of *sarma* that is eaten hot, but that one usually contains meat. The hot, non-vegan *sarma* are also known as *dolma*.

Lokum - known as Turkish delight to English speakers, this gel-like confection is traditionally made with corn starch, not gelatin, and so is naturally vegan. There are many different types of *lokum*, but the classic one is cut into cubes, flavored with rosewater, orange or lemon, and dusted with powdered sugar.

Fancier varieties will contain chopped nuts and/or dates that are bound up inside the gel. This type of sweet is popular throughout the Middle East and in Greece but is said to have originated in Turkey. The name *lokum* is derived from a phrase in Arabic that translates roughly as "comfort for the throat".

Cezerye - the name of this sweet is derived from the Arabic word for "carrot", and that's because this semi-gelatinous confection is made from caramelized carrots, along with shredded coconut and nuts. You may find some variations that replace the carrot with fig or date purée.

Cezerye is a relatively healthy dessert, as it uses only natural sweeteners. It's especially popular in the southern city of Mersin, where it is believed to be an aphrodisiac. It is usually cut into rectangular blocks the size of a matchbox and served at special occasions.

Vegan Food in Turkish Restaurants outside Turkey

Outside of Turkey, the majority of Turkish restaurants take the form of meat-based kebab joints. This is unfortunate, because kebab is actually just one of many dishes eaten in Turkey and is certainly not the be all and end all of Turkish cuisine.

These kebab houses do have one advantage for vegans, however: they almost always serve *falafel*! As I mentioned earlier, falafel is *not* a traditional Turkish food, and many people in Turkey have never heard of it.

Somehow, though, it has become a key fixture on kebab shop menus outside of Turkey. This is great news for vegans and vegetarians, as these kebab shops are now one of the most popular forms of international fast food and are easy to find in many countries throughout the world.

Generally, a portion of falafel includes four or more chickpea fritters and is served either in a pita pocket, in a wrap, or on a plate with salad and other accompaniments.

The wrap version is known as a *dürüm*. The sauce served with falafel is usually made from tahini (sesame seed paste) and may or may not have yogurt added to it, so it's best to ask. If you're at a kebab shop where the standard sauce is not vegan, ask if they can use plain tahini instead.

While falafel is definitely the most common vegan offering at kebab shops, you will sometimes find other vegan dishes, such as a bean or lentil soup. And if for some reason they don't have falafel, they should be able to make you a pita or *dürüm* wrap stuffed with lettuce, tomatoes, onions, some pickled vegetables and some French fries. It's not gourmet cuisine, but it'll do in a pinch!

Some kebab shops also serve *lahmacun* and/or *pide*, both of which are often considered to be the Turkish equivalent of pizza.

While *lahmacun* traditionally includes meat, either one can be made with just veggies, at least in theory. A few kebab shops have started trying their hand at Italian-style pizza as well, so at those places, you could always order a veggie pizza without the cheese.

One advantage of kebab stands is that they are often open late at night or on weekends and holidays when other eateries are closed.

They are commonly found in European countries such as the Netherlands, thanks to the Turkish workers who immigrated in past decades to fill the gaps in the workforce. The Europeanized menu at these places often includes meatless *lahmacun* to meet the growing demand for vegetarian and vegan options in Europe.

If you're lucky, you might come across a Turkish restaurant that is not just a kebab shop and that actually offers a full menu of Turkish dishes. Back in 2006, I lived in Doha, Qatar, where there's a fantastic restaurant called Turkey Central.

It's nothing fancy, but it offers an extensive menu, including a meze platter with many different spreads and other dishes served with bread.

My work colleagues and I used to go there a lot, because the platters were great for sharing with a group of people. I wasn't vegan back then, but looking back now I realize that almost those meze we ate were vegan. If I ever find myself in Doha again, Turkey Central will be the first restaurant I visit.

Extra Resources

Culinary Backstreets is a company that offers culinary walks in about a dozen cities around the world. On request, they can offer a completely vegan version of their tour through

Istanbul's historic district of Beyoğlu, which includes visits to pickle makers and other artisans.

Ahara Vegan and Yoga Hotel in Kizilot made history when it opened in November 2016 as the first 100 percent vegan hotel on the Turkish Riviera. They offer yoga sessions for all levels, as well as other activities like meditation, massage, and a Turkish bath. The restaurant focuses on the naturally vegan dishes that are part of traditional Turkish cuisine.

Kartepe Farm Animal Sanctuary is located in Anatolia, about 100 kilometers from Istanbul. It aims to protect farm animals from cruelty, inspire change in the way society views and treats farm animals, and promote compassionate vegan living. They welcome visitors and volunteers. Also in Kartepe is the Raw Gourmets International Culinary Arts and Hospitality Institute, run by Turkey's top raw chef, Mehmet Ak. The Institute teaches classes and workshops and also offers accommodation.

The Turkish Vegan and Vegetarian Association has a website that's only in Turkish, but if you contact them they could provide useful information about local events, such as the Didim Vegfest organized in April 2017. They can be reached at tvd@tvd.org.

Vegan in Turkey! is a Facebook group where you can connect with local vegans in Turkey. There's also a group called *RAW/VEGAN FOOD TURKEY*, which is focused more on raw diets, and there are smaller groups for vegans in specific Turkish cities.

Chapter Six

Indian Cuisine

Vegan Food in India

Earlier, when we talked about Chinese cuisine, I referred to China as the birthplace of veganism. And while I still stand by that statement, it's certainly true that the practice of non-violence that developed among Buddhist monks in China was rooted in an even longer Indian tradition.

Hinduism, Jainism, and Buddhism all originated in India, and they all have *ahimsa* (non-violence) at the core of their teachings. While the number of practicing Buddhists has certainly declined in the land where the religion originated (apart from in the city of Dharamsala, where the Dalai Lama and many of his followers live in exile), Hinduism and Jainism together are practiced by more than a billion people in India.

And since both these religions advocate a lactovegetarian diet, about 40 percent of India's total population is vegetarian. Thus, as you can imagine, the cuisine is loaded with vegetable-based dishes. Every Indian restaurant you walk into is guaranteed to have an extensive vegetarian section as part of its menu.

The first time I visited India, back in 2004, I essentially became vegetarian for the four months that I was there. Even though I did not yet understand the ethics of eating animals, I just didn't see any reason to eat meat when there were so many delicious vegetarian dishes to choose from. The veggie meals were also cheaper than the meat-based dishes, and I was backpacking on a very tight budget at the time.

Plus, I was worried about getting sick (Delhi belly is a very real phenomenon), and I figured that eating vegetarian food would be safer than eating meat. And in my experience, that turned out to be true. When celebrating my 28th birthday in India, I decided that I would splurge on some international food, so I ordered chicken burritos at a restaurant catering to foreign tourists. I was very sick that night! I quickly went back to eating vegetarian curries from restaurants where the locals eat, and there were certainly plenty of those to choose from.

You won't have to worry about hidden ingredients such as lard, gelatin or meat stock, either. These ingredients are not used in traditional Indian cuisine, and in any case, restaurant owners are very attuned to the needs of their vegetarian customers and are careful to keep their veg and non-veg offerings separate.

In addition to mainstream restaurants, vegetarian and "pure vegetarian" restaurants abound in India. The terms "veg" and "pure veg" as used in India can be a bit confusing for foreigners, though, so here's what they mean:

In India, eggs are generally *not* considered to be part of a vegetarian diet. Thus, any food that is marked as vegetarian is guaranteed to be free of meat and meat-derived products, and also free of eggs.

And such labeling is actually required by law in India, so all packaged food products carry a symbol to show whether they are vegetarian or non-vegetarian. The vegetarian symbol is a green circle inside a green square, while the non-vegetarian symbol is a brown circle inside a brown square.

Some restaurants will go further by calling themselves "pure veg" or "pure vegetarian". It is important to realize, however, that this is *not* the same as vegan. "Pure veg" generally means that the food does not contain any garlic or onion, and perhaps other root vegetables such as potatoes.

Cow's milk is still fair game, however, as is honey. And while honey is not used very much in Indian cuisine, milk products most definitely are, at least in the regional cuisine of northern India.

Despite the importance of *ahimsa* as a central tenet of Indian religions, the exploitation of cows for their milk is deeply rooted in Indian culture. Most Indians believe that cows in the domestic dairy industry are well cared for, and they are unaware of the horrors inflicted on the pregnant and lactating cows and their calves. Veganism is thus not (yet) widely understood by Indians, although in recent years this has started to change.

Organizations such as Vegan Outreach have begun running awareness-raising and leafleting campaigns throughout the country. As a result, more and more Indians are realizing that the consumption of milk is not in line with their values of compassion and non-violence.

For the time being, though, you'll still need to ask a few questions about milk and its derivatives when ordering food in India. While hard cheese is not very common, many dishes contain cream, yogurt (known as "curd"), clarified butter (known as "ghee"), or a soft cheese called "paneer".

You may not be understood if you just ask for "no dairy products", so it's a good idea to list out all the ingredients that you want to avoid, just to be safe.

100

On the plus side, southern Indian cuisine is much more likely to use coconut milk than cow's milk. While northern Indian dishes can often be veganized with just a little adaption, there are a number of southern Indian dishes that are already naturally vegan and don't require any changes at all.

And throughout the country, lentils and other legumes (known collectively as "*dal*") and whole grains in the form of *roti* (a flatbread) are staples of the Indian diet.

Cristina Luisa, who blogs at Chronicles of a Travel Addict, found that avoiding dairy products was the only real challenge she faced when ordering vegan food in India. Here's Cristina's advice to vegan travelers in India, in her own words:

"While you will get plenty of confused head-nods and raised eyebrows when you utter the word 'vegan,' this doesn't mean that traveling in India on a purely plant-based diet is impossible. There might be a couple of hiccups due to language barriers, and you may have to send a couple of plates back, but overall, being vegan in India is definitely doable.

First off, prepare yourself to repeat the words "No milk, no butter, no cheese" repeatedly like it's a mantra. Saying "no dairy" can be open to interpretation, which might lead to having chunks of paneer in your otherwise perfect medley of veggie dishes. Get to know the local dishes and their ingredients beforehand. Find out which rice and which chapati are safe to eat. Oftentimes, there are accidentally vegan (and absolutely delicious) dishes, like dosa masala, made from rice. Coconut milk is often used as well, but be sure to ask beforehand to clarify. Most of the time, creamy food has cow's milk in it.

With a bit of research, a lot of patience, and adaptability (forget about your soy lattes; you're drinking that coffee black), traveling in India as a vegan can be quite simple. There are so many lovely vegetable dishes to choose from- like aloo gobi, channa masala, and dal- that you will never feel deprived or lacking in nutrients. Just be sure to plan ahead when taking long train or bus rides, because most of the accessible "veggie" food can be questionable. Banana chips, nuts, bread, and fruit- not to mention bottled water- are life savers."

Vegan or Veganizable Dishes to Seek Out

Pakoras - this word is used to describe a variety of vegetable-based fried snacks or appetizers, and what exactly a *pakora* is depends on where in India you are. In some parts of the country, "*pakora*" can refer to any food (usually a vegetable) that has been dipped in chickpea flour and fried.

Some common vegetables used to make *pakoras* include potatoes, spinach, cauliflower, and onions.

In other parts of the country, *"pakora"* refers to a mix of chopped onions, green chilies, and spices mixed in chickpea flour. In these regions of the country, the vegetable fritters known elsewhere as *"pakoras"* are called *"bajji"* instead.

Chana masala - this chickpea curry is popular in northern India, although it's also eaten as a breakfast food in the southern state of Kerala. In addition to chickpeas, the usual ingredients include onion, chopped tomatoes, coriander seeds, garlic, chilies, and *garam masala* spice mix.

Traditionally, the type of chickpea used is the one known in India as *chana* or *kala chana*, which is much smaller and firmer than the chickpeas typically eaten in Western countries (which are called *chole* in India). In restaurants, however, *chana* may be replaced with the larger *chole*.

Dal - this is a broad term that is used in India to refer to pulses in general - which includes all kinds of lentils, peas, and beans - as well as the soups prepared with these pulses. It is one of the most important staple foods in India and neighboring countries and is typically eaten with either *roti* (flatbread) or rice.

It often appears on restaurant menus in the form of "*dal tarka*" or "*dal tadka*". To prepare this dish, a mix of spices is fried in oil along with ginger, garlic, and onions and then poured over the cooked *dal*, which is usually yellow split pigeon peas.

Sambar - this is the form in which *dal* is most often prepared in southern India. It is essentially a lentil soup or stew that is flavored with tamarind. While it can be served as a main course with rice, it is also often served as a side dish to accompany other dishes, such as *dosa* and *idli* (see descriptions of these below).

Baingan bharta - this dish is sometimes compared to *baba ghanoush* (a cold dip eaten in the Middle East). While they are both made with grilled eggplant that has been mashed into a purée, *baingan bharta* is served hot with *roti* and rice, much like other Indian curry dishes. The two dishes do, however, both have a smoky flavor, thanks to the grilling of the eggplant.

Aloo gobi - "*aloo*" means "potato" and "*gobi*" means "cauliflower", so this is a dish of potatoes and cauliflower mixed with Indian spices. There are many variations of this common dish, which can be served either "dry" (with very little liquid) or "wet" (with lots of sauce).

There are many other Indian dishes made with these two common ingredients in combination with other vegetables. For example "*aloo matar*" is a dish of potatoes and peas, and you might even find all three together, potato, peas, and cauliflower, which would be called "*aloo gobi matar*".

Masala dosa - a *dosa* is a very thin crêpe or pancake made from a fermented batter of lentils and rice. To make a *masala dosa*, the *dosa* is then stuffed with a spicy potato mixture and served with a variety of chutneys. This dish traditionally comes from the south of India, but it can now be found throughout the country.

Idli - this savory, steamed cake is a popular breakfast food in southern India. Like *dosas*, *idlis* are made from a batter of fermented lentils and rice. Eaten alone, the *idli* has a very mild taste. It is almost always served with *sambar*, however, and with different types of chutneys.

Roti - also known as *chapati*, this whole grain flatbread is an integral part of Indian cuisine. It is an unleavened bread, unlike *naan*, which is leavened with yeast. *Naan* is usually made with yogurt, however, whereas *roti* is always vegan.

Sometimes curries are eaten with both rice and *roti*, but it's also common to forego the rice and just use a piece of *roti* to scoop up the curry. Remember to only use your right hand when eating this way, though. Like in Ethiopia and in many other countries in Africa and the Middle East, eating with the left hand is taboo in India.

Kadai mushroom - this is a dish of button mushrooms served in a gravy of spicy tomato sauce with green bell peppers. A *"kadai"* is a multi-purpose pan found in every Indian kitchen. It's similar to a Chinese wok, but much deeper. This is a one-pot dish cooked entirely in the *kadai*, which is why it's referred to as *"kadai mushroom"*. If you see the more common *"kadai paneer"* dish on a restaurant menu, try asking if they can replace the *paneer* with mushrooms to make this vegan version of the dish.

Disclaimer: While many of these dishes are always prepared exclusively with vegan ingredients, variations abound, and some cooks might use *ghee* (clarified butter) for frying instead of oil, or they might add cream to the sauce. These ingredients can usually be omitted upon request, but it's important to clarify that you want your dish without any dairy products. The best way to get your point across is probably by rattling off the names of the milk products commonly used in India, such as *ghee*, yogurt, *paneer*, and cream.

Vegan Food in Indian Restaurants outside India

The selection of food available in Indian restaurants outside of India may be somewhat different from the selection in a typical restaurant in India, but there will still be plenty of vegetarian offerings, some of which will be vegan or veganizable.

The differences between Indian restaurants inside and outside India emerge mainly in the sections of the menu that contain meat dishes. For one, these sections are often larger than they would be in India. Also, they will include beef dishes - something you won't find in most restaurants in India, apart from in certain states like Kerala, or in areas with large Muslim populations.

Even McDonald's in India has attempted to avoid upsetting either the Hindu or the Muslim community by keeping beef as well as pork off their menu. In Indian restaurants abroad, though, all types of meat are fair game.

Certain countries with large Indian immigrant communities have developed their own particular form of Indian cuisine, sometimes inventing completely new dishes. For example, a "*balti*" is a style of curry that is thought to have originated in Birmingham, England.

And in South Africa, the Indian community in the city of Durban has created an unusual dish known as "bunny chow". This consists of a hollowed out loaf of bread that is then filled with curry and eaten with the hands.

But even if some of the dishes on the menu would be unfamiliar to people in India, there's one thing that's a constant feature of almost any Indian restaurant: a vegetarian section of the menu.

This makes it easy because you can ignore all the other parts of the menu and just flip straight to the vegetarian section. From there, ask your server which dishes are already devoid of milk products and which can be adapted to be vegan.

This will vary by restaurant, so it's impossible to say that any particular dish is always or almost always vegan by default. Some restaurants might cook their dishes in *ghee*, while others will use oil instead. Even obviously non-vegan dishes like *dal makhani* (mungo beans and kidney beans cooked in butter and cream) can often be made vegan on request.

In some curry houses in the UK, you may find that the menu is set up a bit differently. Instead of dividing the menu by the main ingredient (beef, chicken, pork, vegetables, etc.) they will instead list all the different types of curries they offer. These will have names like *jalfrezi*, *dopiaza*, Madras, etc.

The menu will then state that any of the curries can be made with the meat of your choice *or* with vegetables.

In this case, you just need to ask which dishes can be made without dairy or eggs. Odds are, most of them can be, apart from a few sauces such as *korma* that contain yogurt or cream as an integral ingredient.

In addition to the main dishes, there will also be some veggie appetizers such as *pakoras* or *samosas*, and these are often vegan as well. And then, of course, there are the standard accompaniments, like rice, *roti*, and *papadums*.

While it might take a bit of effort to make it understood that you don't eat dairy, once you make it over that hurdle, Indian cuisine has a plethora of great vegan options to offer.

Extra Resources

Veg Voyages. If you want to experience the wonders of India but would prefer to leave the planning to someone else, this vegan tour company runs a number of different vegan tours to the country, ranging in length from 8 to 16 days.

Veggie Hotels lists more than 70 hotels, resorts, and other accommodation options in India that serve only vegetarian food in their restaurants. If you are interested in a yoga retreat, ayurvedic treatments, or another type of relaxing getaway, try contacting one of these places to see what vegan options they offer. Those that have been recommended as being particularly vegan-friendly include Shreyas Retreat in Bangalore, Erandia Marari Ayurveda Beach Resort in Kerala, and Kairali Ayurvedic Healing Village, also in Kerala.

Vegans in India is one of the many Facebook groups where you can connect with vegans living in India. There are lots of smaller niche groups too, including a group for vegans with cats and dogs, a group for pro-intersectional vegans, and even a matchmaking group for vegans looking for a vegan spouse.

And if you'd like to recreate the delicious flavors of Indian cuisine in your own home, there are a few recipe books devoted to vegan Indian cooking that have received high praise:

Vegan Richa's Indian Kitchen by popular blogger and recipe developer Richa Hingle.

The Indian Vegan Kitchen: More Than 150 Quick and Healthy Homestyle Recipes by Madhu Gadia

Vegan Indian Cooking: 140 Simple and Healthy Vegan Recipes by Anupy Singla

As for finding recipes on the Internet, a great place to start is *Holy Cow! Vegan Recipes*. This blog is written by Vaishali, who is of Indian origin but now lives and cooks in Washington, D.C. and shares recipes from India as well as American and other cuisines.

Chapter Seven

Italian Cuisine

Vegan Food in Italy

There is a common misconception that Italian food is all about meat and cheese. Especially cheese. In reality, this couldn't be further from the truth. Authentic, traditional, Italian fare is largely plant-based, at least in many regions of the country.

Like Chinese cuisine, Italian cuisine varies tremendously from one region to another, and sometimes even from one village to the next. In fact, Massimo Montanari, an eminent scholar in the field of food studies, has argued that there is no such thing as "Italian cuisine". And indeed, it does seem rather meaningless to lump together such a vast range of ingredients and cooking styles into a single category.

Thanks to this great regional diversity, there are hundreds of vegan or easily veganizable dishes in the Italian cooking tradition. However, regional diversity means, of course, that many of these dishes are only found within a certain region, which makes it difficult to give general recommendations about which dishes to seek out. In the next section of this chapter, I will list a few of the more common dishes that can be found in multiple regions, or in some cases all throughout the country.

But please keep in mind that this is just the tip of the iceberg, and that, depending on exactly where in Italy you are, there will be plenty of lesser-known, local specialties to discover. Italy holds a very special place in my heart; my husband and I met there in 2001 when I was working in Rome as a tour guide, and then in 2007 we returned there to get married. We try to get back to Italy as often as we can, and we have spent lots of time exploring the lesser-known destinations that don't fit into most visitors' itineraries.

And in 2018 I will be putting my tour guide hat back on and leading a small group of veggie lovers on a vegan tour of Rome, Bologna and Lucca! For more information on this tour as well as other vegan tours I'll be leading, contact Kim at Veg Jaunts and Journeys and ask about upcoming itineraries.

In my next book, *Italy for Veggie Lovers*, I will go into much greater detail about the cuisine in each of Italy's 20 regions and describe a number of specialty dishes that are specific to each region. *Italy for Veggie Lovers* will be released in 2018, but you can get a sneak peek at one of the chapters by downloading it for free at: thenomadicvegan.com/veganitaly

When it comes to regional variations, the south is definitely the most vegan-friendly part of the country. The regions of Sicily, Apulia, Basilicata and Campania, in particular, are a veggie lover's paradise, as Kati Tímár discovered during her travels around Sicily:

"I had the most amazing culinary experiences while traveling in Sicily. I ate the best pizza ever in a small restaurant on the edge of Taormina (I think it was called "La Trattoria da Ugo"). The topping was only tomato sauce and very soft roasted eggplant. I still keep thinking about it. In fact, it is very easy to eat out in Italy as a vegan. Even if the dish that you would like contains cheese on the menu, you can ask the waiter for a version without it.

What I love about Sicily is that fruit and vegetables, such as oranges and tomatoes have very intense flavors. I sometimes think that there should be other words used for these veggies because they are so much tastier than anything we can find in northern parts of Europe. And I was often stunned to see how cheap they are."

Central regions such as Umbria, Le Marche, Lazio, and Tuscany produce excellent cereals and legumes and have plenty to offer vegan visitors as well.

For example, the most famous lentils in Italy, *le lenticchie di Castelluccio*, are produced in Umbria. Tuscany has an abundance of bean-based dishes. In fact, Italians from other parts of Italy refer to people from Tuscany as "*i toscani mangiafagioli*", which means "the Tuscan bean-eaters".

It's only when you reach the far north of the country, where the mountainous terrain is more conducive to the grazing of livestock than the planting of crops, that local vegan specialties become a bit thin on the ground. But don't worry; you can easily find a good meal even in the remote mountain villages of Val d'Aosta.

In order to quickly spot the vegan offerings on a restaurant menu in Italy, it helps to know how an Italian menu is laid out. Basically, it's divided up into courses. First come the *antipasti* (appetizers), followed by the *primi* (first course dishes), the *secondi* (second course dishes), and finally the *dolci* (desserts). There will also be a section listing the *contorni* (side dishes), which need to be ordered separately.

Most of the vegan options will be hanging out in the *antipasti*, *primi* and *contorni* sections of the menu. You can pretty safely skip over the *secondi* section, as the second course is traditionally a meat or fish dish. That being said, restaurants are becoming aware of the growing demand for vegan options, and some are adding vegan items such as smoked seitan to their list of *secondi* dishes.

The dessert section will probably include some fresh fruit and not much else that's vegan. But that's not a problem, because you can always head to the nearest *gelateria* after your meal for some delicious homemade ice cream that will be just bursting with flavor. If you've never had authentic Italian *gelato* before, you're in for a real treat! I'll tell you more about it in the next section.

Vegan or Veganizable Dishes to Seek Out

Bruschetta - a popular appetizer of toasted garlic bread that can come with a wide variety of different toppings, including some vegan ones. One of the most common toppings is diced tomatoes, sometimes served with the addition of fresh basil leaves.

There are a few other toppings that may be vegan, and indeed often are, but you will need to ask to be sure. These include a number of different creamy sauces which, despite the word *"crema"* in their name, usually don't contain any cream. These types of *crema* are more like a paste or purée, and they can be made from artichoke hearts (*crema di carciofi*), eggplant (*crema di melanzane*), or any number of other vegetables.

Crema di olive is another popular *bruschetta* topping and is similar to the tapenade found in southern France. In this case, the non-vegan ingredient to watch out for is not cheese but anchovies. But again, not all cooks will add this, so just ask your server. You can also order a simple *bruschetta bianca*, which is just toasted bread rubbed with garlic and drizzled with olive oil, with no other toppings.

Verdure grigliate - commonly served as a side dish or appetizer, this is simply a plate of grilled vegetables, which is always a healthy and delicious option. The vegetables will mostly likely include eggplant, zucchini, and bell peppers, although in the north you may come across grilled onions or even potatoes in the mix.

Focaccia - this delicious, spongy bread can be topped with a number of different vegetables, herbs, and spices (and sometimes also cheese and other non-vegan ingredients). In its most basic form, it's flavored with nothing more than coarse salt and olive oil.

A basic *focaccia* is similar to an Italian pizza base, and in fact, there's really not much difference between a *focaccia* and a *pizza bianca,* at least when purchased in a bakery or a place that sells pizza by the slice to take away. In a more formal pizzeria, *pizza bianca* (literally "white pizza") may refer to any kind of pizza that does not come with tomato sauce, and sometimes you'll see pizza menus divided into sections titled *"pizze bianche"* (white pizzas) and *"pizza rosse"* (red pizzas).

But getting back to *focaccia,* rosemary and tomatoes are popular toppings, and the variations and combinations are limitless. The region of Liguria is particularly famous for its *focaccia*. There, it's often available in Italian bars (which are really more like snack counters than drinking dens), and it makes a convenient on-the-go lunch or between-meal snack. But even within this one region, the texture and flavor of *focaccia* vary tremendously, from soft and oily to as hard and crunchy as a cracker. In Florence, *focaccia* with rosemary and potatoes is popular. And in Apulia, the *focaccia* you will find most often is *barese* ("Bari-style"), which is topped with cherry tomatoes, olives, oregano, salt and olive oil.

Caponata - commonly served as a side dish, but also sometimes appearing as an appetizer or even as a main course, Sicilian *caponata* is a vegetable stew in a sweet and sour sauce flavored with sweetened vinegar. Eggplant always features prominently, and there are usually some capers thrown into the mix, but the rest of the ingredients can vary.

Some cooks will add olives, carrots and bell peppers, while others will use potatoes, or even raisins and pine nuts. Note that, while the Sicilian version of *caponata* is vegan and is the one that's most widely known, other (non-vegan) versions do exist. In Naples, for example, *caponata* is made with mozzarella cheese and sometimes tuna or anchovies.

Penne all'arrabbiata - this spicy pasta dish is usually made with penne pasta, but you might also see the same sauce served with spaghetti. In any case, both of these pasta shapes are dried pasta, as opposed to fresh, and are normally made without eggs. The word *"arrabbiata"* translates as "angry" and refers to the fiery kick to the sauce, which is made with tomatoes, garlic, chili pepper, and parsley.

Penne all'arrabbiata is sometimes eaten with grated Pecorino cheese, so you might want to say *"senza formaggio"* (without cheese) when you place your order. This is a typical Roman dish, but it can also be found on menus in many other places across the country. Like so many Italian dishes, it's made with just a few simple ingredients of the highest quality.

Pasta e fagioli - this hearty stew of pasta and beans is an extremely popular dish in traditional Italian cuisine. It should come as no surprise, though, that each region has put its own spin on it. In Umbria, for example, the local variation is called *pasta e fagioli allo zafferano* and is infused with saffron - a highly-sought-after spice that has been cultivated in the region since at least the thirteenth century and appears in many local dishes.

It's best to inquire about the exact ingredients of *pasta e fagioli*, because not all versions are vegan. The type made in Napoli almost always is, but in Bologna, for example, it's made with prosciutto.

Spaghetti aglio olio e peperoncino - this is another one of those very simple dishes in Italian cuisine that relies on fresh, high-quality ingredients to really make the flavors pop. It consists of nothing more than spaghetti tossed with small red chili peppers and garlic that has been lightly sautéed in olive oil.

The dish can be made even simpler (and milder) by leaving out the chili peppers, in which case it's just called "*spaghetti aglio olio*". It's often sprinkled with parsley before serving. The recipe used in the southern region of Basilicata is distinctive because it calls for dried sweet peppers (*peperoni cruschi*) that have been ground up into a powder. This adds a red tint and a unique flavor to the dish.

Pasta alla norma - this dish originated in the city of Catania in Sicily and is supposedly named after the opera *Norma*, written by Catania-born composer Vincenzo Bellini. The sauce is a simple combination of tomato and basil, with the addition of chunks of eggplant. Cheese is often grated over the top, so just ask for it without (*senza formaggio*). While it's definitely a Sicilian specialty, its popularity has spread to other parts of the country.

Pizza marinara - this was the very first pizza ever invented, and it was the creation of an unknown baker working in the back streets of Naples in the eighteenth century. The name is the source of some confusion, as many people mistakenly believe that it's a seafood pizza. In fact, some restaurants outside Italy (or even occasionally in other regions of Italy) make the same mistake, so be sure to check the ingredients listed on the menu.

If it's an authentic pizza marinara, there will be no sea creatures on it, and also no cheese! This is pizza in its purest and simplest form, topped with nothing but tomato sauce, garlic and dried oregano, and maybe a little salt and pepper. It's one of the most popular types of pizza in Italy and features on the menu of just about every pizzeria in the country. It might sound plain, and if the quality of the ingredients or the skills of the *pizzaiolo* who make it are not up to scratch, then yeah, it can be a bit underwhelming. But when made by a Neapolitan *pizzaiolo* using fresh, high-quality ingredients, it's astounding.

I recently spent a few days in Naples and took the opportunity to seek out the best pizza marinara in the city. While I didn't have time to try *all* of Naples' pizzerie, I did eat five pizze marinare in four days! For what it's worth, my favorite was the pizza from Il Figlio del Presidente on Via Duomo.

Gelato - Italian *gelato* is some of the best ice cream in the world, and most *gelaterie* will offer vegan options. The fruit flavors are generally sorbets made with nothing but fresh fruit, water, and sugar. The dark chocolate flavor is dairy-free and often vegan as well, though some places do add egg yolks. And, in response to increasing demand, many *gelaterie* are now offering other *gelato* flavors, such as pistachio, that are made with soy milk or other plant-based milks. Some ice cream cones are accidentally vegan, but if not you can just have it in a cup instead.

Vegan Food in Italian Restaurants outside Italy

Outside of Italy, and particularly in the United States, Italian restaurants do tend to go a bit heavier on the meat and cheese to satisfy local tastes. Nevertheless, they are sure to have at least a few items that are vegan or can easily be veganized.

123

Bruschetta with diced tomatoes is a great option for an appetizer, and many places will also offer an *antipasti* buffet or a large platter of grilled vegetables.

Any pizza can be ordered without cheese, and *pizza marinara* is already cheese-free by default. There will often be a vegetarian pizza on the menu, but if not you can just ask for toppings such as mushrooms, eggplant, zucchini, bell peppers, and even pineapple. The crust should be vegan if it's made according to a traditional recipe, but it's worth asking. With all the stuffed crust pizzas and other bastardizations of Italian cuisine out there, you just never know, and recipes for pizza dough can change from country to another.

Plus, the international pizza chains are constantly changing their recipes, so what was vegan last year may not be vegan this year. Currently, at Pizza Hut, the Thin N' Crispy and Hand-Tossed crusts are vegan, but some others aren't. For the full lowdown on all the vegan items available at major chain restaurants, download the handy Vegan Xpress smartphone app.

While fresh pasta will probably contain eggs, most types of dried pasta should be vegan, and almost any Italian restaurant will have some form of egg-free pasta.

124

You can ask for it with a simple tomato sauce (*al pomodoro*), or with the spicier version, *all'arrabbiata*. Both of these are commonly available in Italian restaurants outside Italy, and even if you don't see them on the menu, the kitchen staff should be able to whip up these simple dishes on request.

Even Olive Garden, which in many ways represents the very worst of Americanized Italian food (they serve fried lasagna, for crying out loud!), has spaghetti with a vegan tomato sauce. Granted, it's only on the kid's menu, but it's there.

And in fact, other types of restaurants that are not at all vegan-friendly, such as ski lodges in the French or Swiss Alps, will often offer *spaghetti al pomodoro* or *spaghetti all'arrabbiata* as their token vegetarian dish.

Extra Resources

Italy for Veggie Lovers is the title of my next book, which will be released in 2018. We've barely scratched the surface in this chapter. If you want the full low-down, *Italy for Veggie Lovers* will offer a much more in-depth look at Italian food through a vegan lens. Sign up at thenomadicvegan.com/veganitaly to get advance access to the first chapter and be notified as soon as the book is published.

In the meantime, if the recipes described here sound tempting, but you aren't planning a trip to Italy anytime soon, don't despair. Many Italian recipes are ridiculously easy and simple, so why not try making them yourself? Here are some recommended recipe books:

Vegano Italiano: 150 Vegan Recipes from the Italian Table by Rosalba Gioffré. Originally published in Italian and now also available in an English translation.

Nonna's Italian Kitchen: Delicious Home-Style Vegan Cuisine by Bryanna Clark Grogan

Vegan Italiano: Meat-free, Egg-free, Dairy-free Dishes from Sun-Drenched Italy by Donna Klein

Vegan Travel Club (formerly *Vegano Italiano Tours*) run all-inclusive tours to Sicily and to the Amalfi-Cilento coast, which are two of the most vegan-friendly destinations in all of Italy. And on the tour, you may even have the chance to rub elbows with vegan celebrities like vegan cheesemaker extraordinaire, Miyoko Schinner.

Veg Jaunts and Journeys 2018 Italy Tour – This is a tour that I will be leading personally! Join me as we eat our way through Bologna, Rome and Lucca, while discovering Italy's fascinating history, architecture and culture in between bites.

Our visit to Bologna will coincide with VeganFest – the largest vegan event in the world!

Vegan Italy is probably the best Facebook group for connecting with Italian vegans (the larger *Italy for Vegans* group is not very active). There's also an Italian group devoted to vegan yoga and fitness that has a large membership.

Chapter Eight

Mexican Cuisine

Vegan Food in Mexico

Mexican cuisine - and especially the traditional cuisines of its indigenous peoples - is abundant in fresh vegetables, corn, beans, squash, greens, herbs, and seeds. In fact, until the Spanish conquest, most indigenous peoples did not domesticate any animals, which meant that they ate a largely plant-based diet.

The main plant that they cultivated was corn, which they ate at almost every meal. The foundational role of corn in Mexican cuisine is even more important than the role that bread plays in many European cuisines. Whereas bread is a common but optional accompaniment to many European cuisines, without corn, most Mexican dishes simply couldn't be made at all.

The Aztecs and other ancient peoples of Mexico processed the corn by cooking it in an alkaline solution. This increases the corn's nutritional value, but that's just one of the benefits of this process, known as nixtamalization. It also makes it possible to knead the corn into a dough for making tortillas. These form the basis of a number of popular dishes, including *tacos*, *chilaquiles*, and *quesadillas*.

By combining tortillas with beans, squash, and other vegetables, the indigenous peoples of Mexico developed an extremely nutritious, plant-based cuisine. It was the Spanish *conquistadores* who later introduced wheat as well as a number of domesticated animals, including pigs, goats, and cows. As a result, meat and dairy products have now become a major part of modern Mexican cuisine.

They are pretty easy to avoid, however, due to the unique "component" nature of Mexican dishes. Most dishes are made up of several different components (tortillas, rice, tomatoes, lettuce, etc.). This makes them highly adaptable and customizable, so it's easy to pick and choose the components you want to create a vegan version of the dish.

For example, tacos, burritos and even quesadillas can all be made in vegan versions. Just ask to substitute animal products like meat, cheese or sour cream with plant-based alternatives like guacamole, salsa, beans, roasted veggies, chili peppers, etc. It's all about the substitutions.

The basis of the Mexican diet is still corn and beans, with chili pepper used as a seasoning. These are then complemented by the unique flavors of local plants like *huauzontle*, *papaloquelite*, and *nopales*.

The meat is really just the carrier of the spices in Mexican food, and further flavor is then added with condiments like salsa and guacamole. And since beans are everywhere in Mexico and are packed with protein and micro-nutrients, there's really no need for meat to create a filling, nutritious and satisfying meal.

I asked Sam Wood who writes the travel blog Indefinite Adventure about his recent trip to Mexico, and he confirmed that it was easy to mix and match ingredients for a tailor-made vegan meal:

"I was drawn to visit Mexico precisely for its varied, flavorful and healthy cuisine, and, despite some friend's misgivings about me not being able to find vegan food there, I found the cuisine in Mexico to be surprisingly vegan-friendly, precisely because much of it is inherently customizable.

I spent almost three months travelling around the country at the beginning of 2017 and, in my experience, people who work serving food (be it at a food stand on the street or in a nice, sit-down restaurant) were more than happy to substitute one ingredient for another, leave things off the dish or go ask the cook exactly how something was made, for example.

That is to say, it is not uncommon to ask for your dish to be tailored to you when ordering food in Mexico, so this is unlikely to be met with consternation or lack of understanding!

In the big cities and tourist hotspots of Mexico, the concept of veganism is well understood, and people serving food are generally likely to speak good English so communicating what you want shouldn't be a problem. In these places, there is also a lot of overtly vegan food to be found. Indeed, Mexico City has a booming vegan scene and there is growing interest in veganism generally. Almost all cafés there have non-dairy milk alternatives and there are over 25 fully vegan restaurants scattered around the city, with plenty more offering vegan options.

In smaller towns and off the tourist trail, the concept isn't as widely known and, indeed, speaking some Spanish will definitely be useful, just to make sure you end up with what you want. Nonetheless, you'll still undoubtedly be able to easily find something tasty to eat!

One warning regarding spiciness: if you are not used to spicy food, absolutely do not believe Mexicans if they tell you something isn't spicy! Just asking "is this spicy?" is not a helpful way of determining if you're going to be able to enjoy something if you have low spice threshold. Instead, I learnt that asking "would you give this to a child?" gave a more meaningful response, as it made people stop and think for a moment about the objective potency of the food in question."

If you're traveling to Mexico for the first time and have grown up eating what passes for Mexican food in the United States, you're in for a surprise. The Tex-Mex fare that is so popular on the other side of the Río Grande only vaguely resembles the food eaten south of the border.

For one, Tex-Mex is characterized by its heavy use of cheese and meat (especially beef and pork). In Mexico, you will not find cheese melted all over everything, as is so often the case in Mexican restaurants in the United States.

But it's not just a matter of using different ingredients, like the addition of melted cheese. Many of the dishes themselves are different too. Some of the "classic" dishes most commonly associated with Mexican food, such as chili con carne, nachos, and fajitas, are purely Tex-Mex inventions and are nowhere to be found in Mexico.

Instead, you will discover an abundance of authentic Mexican dishes that you've probably never heard of before. In the next section, we'll explore some of the popular Tex-Mex dishes that are also common in Mexico but take somewhat different forms. And I'll also introduce you to a few of the authentic Mexican dishes that are not well known at all outside the country.

In Mexico, lunch is the main meal of the day, and it's usually eaten sometime between 2 p.m. and 4 p.m. Restaurants will often offer a set menu at this time, called the *comida corrida*, which includes a soup, main dish, and dessert. Although the *comida corrida* is popular with travelers on a budget, it's not a good option for vegans, as it's rare for all three courses to be free of animal products.

Instead, a great way to eat cheaply and experience the local food culture is to try out the many street foods on offer. These are collectively known as *antojitos*, which literally means "little cravings". There are dozens if not hundreds of different *antojitos* sold on the streets of Mexico, many of which include corn in some fashion.

In addition to all the *antojitos* made with corn tortillas, corn on the cob is also a popular street food! Just be sure to avoid the non-vegan toppings like sour cream or mayonnaise (a common topping for corn in Mexico) and stick to salt, chili powder or lime juice.

Antojitos are cheap, authentic, and very customizable. Best of all, they are available from early morning to late at night. So, if you're accustomed to eating lunch at 12 p.m., you can do that at a street stall or traditional market instead of having to wait for the restaurants to start serving lunch at 2 p.m.

Many of the dishes described in the next section are *antojitos*, so don't be afraid to practice your Spanish with street vendors and discover the myriad snacks and small dishes they sell.

Vegan or Veganizable Dishes to Seek Out

Sopa azteca - corn tortillas go stale quickly, and this soup's popularity is probably due to the fact that it's a great way to avoid wasting those stale, leftover tortillas. Also known as *sopa de tortilla*, this traditional soup is made with fried pieces of corn tortilla that are added to a broth made with tomatoes, onions, garlic, chili peppers and *epazote* (an herb native to Mexico).

There are a number of optional add-ons that can be served on top of the soup; common vegan options include avocado, *pasilla* chili peppers, lemon juice, olive oil, and more fried tortilla strips. Just be sure to make it known that you don't want any cheese or sour cream added to yours.

Tacos - A soft corn or wheat tortilla folded around a filling. Yep, I said "soft"; the hard taco shells that you find at Taco Bell are an American invention and are unheard of in Mexico.

Some vegan taco options that you might find on menus include: *tacos de rajas* (roasted poblano pepper strips), *tacos de calabaza* (squash), *tacos de papa* (potato), *tacos de flor de calabaza* (squash blossom), *tacos de hongos* (mushroom), *tacos de nopales* (cactus pads), and *tacos de huitlacoche*. The latter is an earthy and sweet black fungus that grows on corn. I realize how weird that sounds, but it's considered a delicacy in Mexico!

Burritos - these stuffed wheat flour tortillas are not as ubiquitous in Mexico as they are in the United States. The fact that they use wheat instead of corn tortillas is a clue that *burrito*s are not strictly a traditional Mexican food, although they are popular in northern towns, particularly in Ciudad Juárez. In central and southern Mexico, they are more commonly referred to as *tacos de harina* ("wheat tacos").

In Mexico, they are usually smaller and thinner than those found north of the border and contain just one or two ingredients. Common vegan fillings include beans, potatoes, rice, and *rajas*.

Quesadillas - even though the word for cheese (*queso*) is in the name of this dish, you can easily ask for yours without cheese. Even the locals sometimes eat them this way.

In Mexico, they are usually made with corn rather than wheat tortillas. Fillings vary but may include *rajas*, squash blossoms, mushrooms, *huitlacoche*, potatoes or other vegetables.

Chilaquiles - a popular breakfast dish made of stale, leftover tortillas cut into small squares to make *totopos* (tortilla chips) and topped with a green or red sauce. The usual toppings are cream, cheese and maybe chicken, but you can leave all this off and just eat the chips and sauce. Some places will offer other toppings such as avocado or beans.

Sopes/huaraches - both *sopes* and *huaraches* consist of fried patties made with corn meal, with toppings added to them. The main difference between the two is their size and shape. *Sopes* are small and round, whereas *huaraches* are larger and more oval, roughly in the shape of a sandal (which is what the word "*huarache*" means in Spanish). Both can be made with plant-based toppings such as beans, *nopales*, onions, potato, salsa and cilantro (otherwise known as coriander).

Tlacoyos - these stuffed corn tortillas are sometimes confused with *huaraches* because they have a similar shape, although the *tlacoyo* is smaller. The cornmeal dough is stuffed with a filling and then flattened out on a griddle. Most traditional *tlacoyo* recipes do not call for lard, and some of the most common fillings are vegan, such as pinto beans or fava beans.

Because they dry out quickly, street vendors often keep them in a covered basket, so don't be shy about asking what's hiding underneath the cover. *Tlacoyos* can come in different colors, depending on the type of corn used to make the dough. It's common to see blue ones, which are made from blue corn kernels. This popular street food is often eaten for breakfast.

Moros y cristianos - the name of this simple dish of rice and beans refers to the centuries of conquest and reconquest as the Moors and Christians fought with each other for control of Spain. The black beans represent the Moors, while the white rice represents the Christians.

Moros y cristianos is probably best known as a Cuban dish, but it is also popular in certain parts of Mexico. This is particularly true in Veracruz, where it is often served with fried plantains and avocado or guacamole. It's usually offered as a side dish, but it can make a filling meal on its own.

Torta - a popular street food, particularly in Mexico City. A *torta* is a flat bread roll stuffed with fillings. Most vendors can make one with beans and whatever veggies they have on hand, such as lettuce, tomato, onion, avocado and hot chili peppers.

Raspado - a slushy made with shaved ice, syrup and fruit. There are many possible flavor combinations, and most are vegan, apart from a few that contain condensed milk or ice cream. One delicious variation is the *chamoyada*, which is a combination of spicy *chamoy* sauce, ice, chili powder, and chunks of mango or apricot.

Churros – deep-fried sticks of pastry dough dusted in powdered sugar and/or cinnamon. These are popular in many Spanish-speaking countries, including Mexico, where they are most commonly eaten for breakfast. Recipes can vary, so it's best to ask about the ingredients to be sure, but traditionally they are made from dough that consists of nothing more than flour, water, salt, sugar and oil.

Vegan Food in Mexican Restaurants outside Mexico

As I've already mentioned, the "Mexican food" sold outside of Mexico is quite different from authentic Mexican food. There's even a proper term for it: Tex-Mex. This is, in fact, a separate cuisine in itself and is loosely based on the food eaten in the far north of Mexico and in the southwestern United States.

While Tex-Mex first became popular in Texas and other southwestern US states, it now seems to have spread across the globe. Not just in the United States but in any country outside of Mexico, this is usually what's served in "Mexican" restaurants.

While the dishes might not be authentic, they still retain their component nature, making it simple to request alterations and substitutions. Beans can easily replace any type of meat, and cheese and sour cream can be replaced with other condiments like guacamole, pico de gallo, salsa verde, etc.

One ubiquitous option is the bean burrito, which is actually one of the top-selling menu items at Taco Bell. Even in its fast-food form, Mexican food is very vegan-friendly. And if you're at Taco Bell and want something a little fancier than a bean burrito, you can ask for the seven-layer burrito without the cheese and sour cream.

In a more upscale Tex-Mex restaurant, fajitas are a good vegan option. Many places will list vegetarian fajitas on the menu anyway, but even if they don't you can ask for them with just the peppers and other veggies, with no meat.Side dishes like corn on the cob can also help to round out your meal.

Extra Resources

Given the popularity of Mexican food in the United States, perhaps it shouldn't come as a surprise that a number of well-respected vegan authors and recipe creators have written Mexican cookbooks. Here are some recommended ones:

The Lotus and the Artichoke ¡Mexico! by Justin P. Moore. Moore combines stories of his own travels in Mexico with recipes that he learned from local cooks or concocted on his own from local ingredients while living in the Mexican seaside town of Lo de Marcos.

Vegan Mexico: Soul-Satisfying Regional Recipes from Tamales to Tostadas by Jason Wyrick offers a deeper look into the history and traditions of Mexican cooking, along with authentic regional recipes like "Oaxacan Black Beans" and "Sonoran Machaca Burritos".

Vegan Tacos: Authentic and Inspired Recipes for Mexico's Favorite Street Food by Jason Wyrick is devoted exclusively to Mexico's favorite antojito - the taco.

¡Salud! Vegan Mexican Cookbook:150 Mouthwatering Recipes from Tamales to Churros by Eddie Garza combines innovative cooking techniques with traditional Mexican staples, creating recipes that are both delicious and healthy.

The Taco Cleanse: The Tortilla-Based Diet Proven to Change Your Life is a tongue-in-cheek parody of all the detoxes and cleanses on the market these days. Guaranteed to prevent or reverse taco deficiency, the book is filled with 75 vegan taco recipes.

Viva Vegan!: 200 Authentic and Fabulous Recipes for Latin Food Lovers by Terry Hope Romero. Together with Isa Chandra Moskowitz, Romero has co-authored some of the most highly revered vegan cookbooks ever published. In her first solo cookbook, Romero, who is Venezuelan-American, covers every aspect of Latin cooking across the Americas, including a number of Mexican recipes.

Decolonize Your Diet: Plant-Based Mexican-American Recipes for Health and Healing by Luz Calvo and Catriona Rueda Esquibel. The authors of this book encourage Mexicans to ditch the fast food and return to their own culture's food roots for both physical health and spiritual fulfillment.

They turn the clock back to introduce readers to the healing properties of the plant-based diet eaten in pre-Hispanic Mexico. This is a vegetarian cookbook that does include recipes with dairy and eggs, but they can easily be omitted or substituted.

Vegan Mexican Food is a website created by the Food Empowerment Project - a wonderful organization that fights for justice for the animals, for farm workers, for communities, and for the planet. The site features plant-based Mexican recipes that have been contributed by food lovers from all over the world.

Dora's Table is a recipe blog run by a Mexican woman named Dora who creates vegan Mexican recipes that stay true to traditional and regional Mexican cuisine. Dora has also written an ebook called Vegan Tamales Unwrapped, which includes recipes for a wide variety of both savory and sweet tamales.

Todo Vegano is a bilingual Spanish/English directory of vegan and vegan-friendly places to eat throughout all of Latin America. It includes a large number of listings for locations in Mexico, including some smaller cities and towns.

There are quite a few Facebook groups for vegans in Mexico, though most of them are geared towards a specific sector of this community. The largest groups seem to be those focused on raw diets, such as *RAW VEGAN MEXICO* and *Superfoods. Vegan. Raw. Organic. México y América Latina.*

Chapter Nine

Middle Eastern Cuisine

Vegan Food in the Middle East

The Middle East is, of course, a vast region, and each country has its own specialties and unique dishes and cooking traditions. Nevertheless, there are a number of core dishes that are well-known throughout the region and that all happen to be vegan.

When referring to Middle Eastern food, I am referring primarily to the food eaten in the countries of the Levant and in Egypt. Of all the countries in the region, these are the ones that travelers are most likely to want to visit, and they are also the ones that have been the most successful in exporting their cuisines to other parts of the world.

Lebanese immigrants, in particular, have done a great job of popularizing their cuisine in Europe, North America and elsewhere, and most of the restaurants that are thought of as Middle Eastern are in fact Lebanese.

The Middle East is actually one of the easiest regions in the world in which to be vegan, though you might not think so at first glance. Grilled meats, such as shish kebab, feature so prominently on restaurant menus that you could be forgiven for thinking that's all the locals eat.

In reality, kebabs are typically a street food or restaurant food, and they are not usually prepared by families at home. Instead, vegetables and legumes are the main staple foods for the vast majority of people in the region.

When eating out, the meat-based dishes are obvious and easy to avoid, and there are many vegan options left to choose from. Most cooking is done with olive oil rather than animal fats, and butter and cream are rarely used, apart from in a few desserts.

As a result, the vegan dishes listed in the next section of this chapter are pretty much always 100 percent vegan. Unlike in many other cuisines, where recipes vary and may or may not include non-vegan ingredients, dishes like hummus, baba ganoush, and tabbouleh are prepared in much the same way throughout the region. The small variations that do occur are largely a matter of exchanging one vegan ingredient for another.

Now, I've already explained why I think it's counter-productive to obsess over small quantities of hidden ingredients like stock or lard, and I stand by that. But if you

146

do want to be extra conscientious about avoiding all traces of animal products, you will be happy to know that this is one cuisine where you can relax and not worry so much about hidden ingredients sneaking their way into your meal.

If you're really grossed out by the thought of lard in your food (and I get it; it grosses me out too), well, you don't have to worry about that in the Middle East. Lard is pig fat, and Muslims don't eat pigs, so any kind of pork product is extremely rare in the region.

That's not to say that everyone in the Middle East is vegan. Far from it. Pigs may be off the menu, but lamb and sheep definitely aren't. The wide variety of vegan dishes in the cuisine is largely the result of geographic and economic factors, rather than the presence of a strong animal rights movement.

In most parts of the region, veganism is not common, so don't expect people to know what the word means. The one major exception to this is in Israel, which has been called "a vegan paradise" and "the global center of veganism" by mainstream media outlets. Israel has more vegans per capita than any other country in the world.

Currently, about five percent of Israelis are vegan, and another eight percent are lacto-ovo vegetarian. So in Israel, not only do you have all the naturally vegan dishes that are part of the local cuisine, you also have a plethora of vegan restaurants, plus all the mainstream restaurants who have added vegan dishes to their menus in response to the large local demand.

Elsewhere in the region, you probably won't see vegan dishes specifically labeled as "vegan" on the menu. But that certainly doesn't mean they aren't there!

Remember the meze of Greece and Turkey? Well, the Middle East has mastered the art of the meze, and many of the vegan dishes of the region fall into this category. Some of them you're probably familiar with already, and they may even be staples in your own kitchen. While meze are typically served as small dishes or appetizers, they can easily be combined together to create a delicious and very filling meal.

My first visit to the region was in 2003, when I traveled overland from Cairo, Egypt to Istanbul, Turkey. On that trip, I stopped in Jerusalem for a couple of weeks and stayed in a hostel inside the walls of the old city. There weren't many dining options in that part of town, especially in the evenings, so I became a regular at the couple of places that did stay open for dinner. This was well before the vegan boom that is now sweeping Israel, but even so most of the meals I ate there consisted of hummus, falafel, and the other meze dishes described in the next section.

Vegan or Veganizable Dishes to Seek Out

Hummus - حُمُّص - a dip or spread made with mashed chickpeas, tahini, olive oil, lemon juice, and garlic. It has become popular in North America and some parts of Europe, and inventive variations on the dish abound. It seems that these days, any dip that contains any kind of legume can be called "hummus".

In Arabic, though, the word "hummus" means "chickpeas", so in the Middle East you won't find any borlotti bean and zucchini hummus, black bean hummus with lime, or any other creative spin on this favorite dish. Instead, you'll find the classic chickpea version, which is often served with whole chickpeas on top and a generous drizzle of olive oil.

Tabbouleh - تبولة - this parsley-based salad originated in the mountains of Syria and Lebanon and has become one of the most popular salads in the Middle East. It's made with finely chopped parsley, tomatoes, mint, bulgur wheat and onions, and seasoned with olive oil, lemon juice, and salt.

Baba ganoush - غنوج بابا - outside of the Middle East, this eggplant and tahini purée is best known by its Lebanese name of *baba ganoush*. In Palestine, a very similar spread is called *mutabbal*, the main difference being that the Palestinian version uses less *tahini*. Along with hummus, this is one of the most famous meze from the Middle East.

The eggplants are grilled whole until the skins become black and blistered, which is what gives the dish its distinctive smoky flavor. Eggplant has long been a feature of Arab cuisine and appears in many recipes. Since the word *"baba"* means "father, it is thought that the name of the dish refers to the lofty position held by the eggplant in the hierarchy of Middle Eastern vegetables.

Fatayer - فطاير - these little savory pies are very popular and can be stuffed either with meat, cheese or spinach. Obviously, it's the spinach one that we're interested in, which is known as "fatayer bi'l-sabanikh". In Lebanon, they are a particular favorite of Christian families during Lent, though they are enjoyed by all communities throughout the region. *Fatayer* are typically served as a meze.

Muhammara - محمرة - this dip made with walnuts, red bell peppers, pomegranate molasses and bread crumbs originated in the city of Aleppo, Syria, though its popularity has spread as far as southeastern Turkey and neighboring countries in the Caucasus. The traditional recipe calls for a particular type of spicy pepper known as the red Aleppo pepper, in addition to the red bell peppers. It has a distinctive crimson hue, and in fact, its name is derived from the Arabic root word for "red". It is eaten as a meze and goes great with warm bread.

Fattoush - فتوش - this bread salad is served in Palestine, Lebanon and elsewhere in the Levant. It belongs to the family of dishes known as *fattat*, in which pieces of stale, toasted or fresh pita flatbread are crumbled and used as the foundation for preparing the dish. Since pita dries out quickly, *fattoush* and other *fattat* dishes are an innovative way of making use of leftover bread that's no longer fresh. The hand-torn pieces of flatbread are toasted or fried until crispy and then tossed with cucumbers, tomatoes, scallions, parsley, wild greens, and lettuce.

Ful medames - مدمس ف ول - this bean dish probably originated in Egypt, and indeed is considered to be Egypt's national dish. Also referred to as just plain old *"ful"* (which just means "beans"), it consists of fava beans stewed and mashed with onions and served with vegetables and greens. Sometimes hard-boiled eggs are served alongside, so ask for it without those. While it is a staple food in Egypt and is commonly eaten for breakfast there, it's also part of the national cuisine of many other Middle Eastern countries.

Falafel - فلافل - these fried patties are often eaten as a street food in the Middle East and throughout the world, though they can also be served as a meze. They are most commonly made with chickpeas, at least in Palestine and Israel, although in Egypt they are usually made from fava beans. Actually, the ones in Egypt go by a different name (*ta'miyya*), and they do occasionally come stuffed with ground meat, so be sure to ask about those.

Elsewhere, *falafel* is a safe bet for vegans. When eaten as a street food, they are wrapped up in pita bread along with chopped onions, cucumbers, garlic, etc. The sauce squirted on top sometimes contains yogurt, but you can ask for plain tahini instead.

Rummaniyeh - الرمانـيه - this delicious Palestinian stew is most commonly associated with the city of Jaffa, but it is also popular in Gaza. The dish is an enticing combination of creamy eggplant, earthy lentils, and sweet pomegranate, with a touch of garlic, olive oil, and lemon juice.

Pomegranate is a highly sought after fruit in the region, as it is regarded as a symbol of abundance and prosperity. This dish makes use of both the fresh fruit itself and pomegranate molasses. In fact, the name *"rummaniyeh"* means "of or like pomegranate".

Manakish - مـناقـيش - a round dough similar to a pizza base, which is baked in the oven and then topped with any number of toppings. Not all toppings are vegan, but the most common one is. It's called *za'atar* and is a condiment made by mixing dried herbs with sesame seeds, sumac, salt and other spices.

Manakish can be sliced into quarters or folded, and they can be eaten for either breakfast or lunch. It's a popular snack or meze in most countries of the Levant. In addition to *za'atar*, other vegan toppings include chili peppers, spinach, or fried eggplant (the latter is especially common in Israel).

Vegan Food in Middle Eastern Restaurants outside the Middle East

Middle Eastern restaurants in other parts of the world usually specialize in Lebanese cuisine, and they offer some great vegan options in the form of meze. In North America, Europe, and other areas with decent-sized vegetarian populations, these restaurants will usually offer a mixed meze platter that is specifically listed as being completely vegetarian.

These vegetarian platters are usually almost entirely vegan, apart from the *labneh* (strained yogurt) that's often included. But it's no problem to simply ask to substitute the *labneh* with an extra helping of one of the other meze included in the platter, such as hummus or *baba ganoush*.

And if you don't see a vegetarian platter on the menu, you can always just order your favorite meze à la carte. Dishes you're likely to see on the meze menu include: falafel, hummus, *baba ganoush*, *fattoush*, tabbouleh, *fatayer*, and perhaps some others not listed here.

In addition to these fancier restaurants that offer full table service, there's another type of eatery that has popularized Middle Eastern food throughout the world: the kebab stand.

If you are looking for a quick and budget-friendly meal on the go, no matter where you are, any kebab stand will offer pita bread stuffed with falafel and fresh salad. The only ingredient to watch out for is the sauce, which might contain yogurt. If it does, you can ask for tahini instead, or even ketchup.

Extra Resources

Ahalan Olympus is an Israeli tour operator that offers a 10-day vegan tour of Israel. In addition to fully vegan meals, the tour also offers the opportunity to pick and eat your own fruit and discover the advanced technology being used to grow food in the desert along what's known as the "Salad Trail". There will also be a chance to meet with members of an Israeli animal rights organization.

Tel Aviv Vegan Food Tour takes you inside the booming vegan culture of Tel Aviv, Israel and helps you navigate the wide selection of vegan options there. On the tour, you will visit four vegan restaurants and also enjoy a tasting at a vegan bakery/ice cream shop.

If you'd like to experiment with Middle Eastern flavors in your own kitchen, these resources will tell you everything you need to know to cook up a storm of meze and other Middle Eastern dishes:

One Arab Vegan - this blog is run by Nada, a vegan who was born into an Egyptian family but grew up in Bahrain, where she still lives. She shares plant-based recipes inspired by Middle Eastern flavors and also writes about what it's like to be a vegan in the Arab world.

Chef in Disguise - this blog is run by Sawsan, a Palestinian woman who grew up in Jordan and now lives in the United Arab Emirates.

She shares authentic Middle Eastern recipes and offers a glimpse into her life as a woman in the Middle East. Sawsan's blog does include non-vegan recipes, but she tags all of her vegan recipes so they are easy to find.

A Lebanese Feast of Vegetables, Pulses, Herbs and Spices - Mona Hamadeh, who grew up in Lebanon and now lives in England, has gathered together recipes from all across Lebanon in this beautifully presented book. And since dairy and eggs are seldom used in Lebanese cuisine, most of the recipes are vegan.

Vegetarian Dishes from Across the Middle East - Originally published in 1983, this book then remained out of print for 20 years.

It is now available once again, and it includes 250 authentic recipes that showcase the vibrant flavors and the healthy variety of plant-based Middle Eastern cooking.

Vegan Food in the Middle East and *Vegans of the Middle East / North Africa* are two Facebook groups where you can connect with vegans in the region.

Chapter Ten

Moroccan Cuisine

Vegan Food in Morocco

Couscous and tajine make up the core of Moroccan cuisine, and since both these dishes are incredibly versatile, vegan versions of them abound. A tajine is literally anything cooked in the ceramic dish known as a ... wait for it ... a tajine!

This deep dish with a conical top is traditionally placed over hot charcoal. Because the cone-shaped lid traps steam and returns the condensed liquid to the pot, only a minimal amount of water is needed to cook in a tajine. As you can imagine, this is very practical when cooking in the Saharan desert.

The dishes known as tajines are slow-cooked, savory stews that often combine both sweet and sour flavors. For example, raisins, prunes, and preserved lemons are common ingredients in tajines. It is this combination of sweet and sour flavors, combined with spices, that give Moroccan tajines their distinctive flavor. In fact, this is true of Moroccan cuisine in general. The four pillars of the Moroccan culinary tradition are said to be sweet, salty, hot, and fruity.

A basic vegetable tajine will typically include a mix of zucchini, carrots, and potatoes, and is usually available in any Moroccan restaurant. The same vegetables also make an appearance in the typical vegetable couscous. Just as a tajine is anything cooked in a tajine pot, a couscous dish is anything served on a bed of couscous.

Couscous is Morocco's national dish and holds great importance for dietary, religious and symbolic reasons. Moroccans believe that it brings God's blessing upon anyone who eats it.

It is a long-standing tradition to eat couscous for lunch on Fridays, and it can be difficult to find a restaurant or café that serves anything else on a Friday afternoon! Often called a grain, couscous is technically more like a pasta. It's made from semolina flour mixed with water, which is rolled by hand into tiny balls.

Typically, a couscous dish is some kind of stew, with a lot of juice to soak into the couscous. But, like with tajines, it could also contain sweet ingredients such as dates, dried apricots, or other dried fruits and nuts. A sweet compote called "*tfaya*" (تفاية), which is made with raisins, caramelized onions, cinnamon and other spices, is a popular accompaniment to serve over couscous.

In addition to the fresh vegetables and the sweetness of the dried fruits and dates, other flavors that you will come across on a daily basis in Morocco include preserved lemons, *harissa*, and *ras al-hanut*. *Harissa* is a red paste that adds a fiery kick to dishes. *Ras al-hanut*, which means "head of the shop" in Arabic, is a complex spice blend that varies from one spice merchant to the next and can contain up to 40 different ingredients.

And lastly, small, thin-skinned lemons are preserved in salt and lemon juice to give a distinctive citrus flavor to tajines and other dishes. Usually, only the rind is used in cooking, because the pulp of the preserved lemon is too salty.

It would be easy to believe that every Moroccan dish is some type of variation on a tajine or couscous. In reality, there's lots more to Moroccan cuisine, but it's not always accessible to foreigners. That's because the best Moroccan food is not found in restaurants.

If you want to experience more of what authentic Moroccan cuisine has to offer, you have three options. First, you could explore the small food stalls that line the streets of Moroccan cities. The street food is excellent, and this is where you'll find dishes like *harira*, *b'ssara*, and *sfenj* (these are all described in the next section).

Your second option is to make friends with the locals and get yourself invited to a Moroccan home for dinner. Of course, there is no guarantee that this will happen, but Moroccans are a very friendly bunch, so you never know. You could try introducing yourself in one of the Moroccan vegan Facebook groups and see what happens.

Finally, your third option is to eat in a *riad* that has been converted into a hotel and/or restaurant. A *riad* is a traditional Moroccan house with an interior courtyard or garden. Typically, the women who work in the kitchens cook the same type of meals that they cook for their own families at home, so *riads* are great places to try authentic Moroccan home cooking. Marrakech has a number of renovated and converted *riads* that now offer accommodation and/or dining for visitors.

In *riads*, you are likely to find an assortment of salads that can be eaten as either appetizers or side dishes. Typically, these are served before the tajine or couscous and then left on the table so diners can continue to enjoy them.

While some Moroccan salads do include lettuce and other raw vegetables, there are also many that are made with cooked vegetables and are what Westerners would probably call a dip or spread rather than a salad. The popular *zaalouk* (described in the next section) is just one example of this type of salad. Given the huge variety of salads available, you could quite easily live just on these alone while in Morocco.

Bread is also ubiquitous; it's eaten at every meal in Morocco, and it's usually vegan. The round loaves called "*khobz*" are the most common type of bread, and they often double as cutlery, as they are used to scoop up salads or tajines.

Vegan or Veganizable Dishes to Seek Out

Kseksu Bidawi (Seven vegetable couscous) - سكس كبع س - خضار - Moroccans consider seven to be a lucky number, so this dish is made with seven vegetables and preferably seven spices. The specific vegetables can vary, but common ones include cabbage, carrots, pumpkin, peas, artichoke hearts, turnips and sweet potatoes. This is the most famous couscous dish in Morocco, and Moroccan families eat it every Friday.

Tajine - الطاجين - these aromatic and fragrantly spiced casseroles are named after the earthenware pot in which they are prepared. Traditionally, tajines were served as a course on their own, with nothing but some bread to dip into the sauce. Nowadays, though, they are often accompanied by a plate of couscous.

161

The possibilities are endless when it comes to the vegetables and fruits used to make the many different kinds of tajine, and it often comes down to which ingredients are readily available. If you travel around Morocco eating tajine every day, you'll probably find that no two tajines are exactly alike.

Zaalouk – زعلوك - a very traditional salad in Morocco, though it's not like the leafy green salads that you might be used to. This one is of the cooked variety and is made with eggplants, tomatoes, and a variety of herbs and spices. It's usually served as a dip with crusty bread.

Loubia – لوبيا - this classic dish is a soup made with white beans cooked in a thick and flavorful tomato sauce. While *loubia* can stand on its own as a main dish, it's sometimes also served at room temperature as a Moroccan salad course. As you've probably figured out by now, the term "salad" has a very broad meaning in Morocco. When served in this way, *loubia* is made extra thick, so that it's more like a dip than a soup.

B'ssara – بيصارة - this puréed dip is similar to hummus, except that it's made with fresh fava beans instead of chickpeas. Added to the puréed beans are garlic paste, cumin, and lemon juice. The purée is used as a dip and eaten with bread. It's also a street food that is sold at small kiosks with bread and tea and eaten either for breakfast or as a snack. And, like *loubia*, it can be either a dip or a soup.

Chermoula - شرمولة - a marinade often used in Moroccan and other North African cuisines. While it's most commonly eaten with fish, it also pairs beautifully with vegetables. There is a dish known as "*hodra mechwya*" that consists of skewered vegetable kebabs basted with *chermoula* and grilled.

The *chermoula* is usually made with a mix of herbs, lemon juice, preserved lemons, oil, garlic, and cumin, but it may include other spices. It can also be mixed with puréed tomatoes to create a sauce that's poured over carrots, green beans or fava beans.

Harira – ال حري رة - a traditional legume-based soup made with lentils, chickpeas, and/or beans. It's commonly served as a starter, but it can also be eaten on its own as a light meal. There are many variations of *harira*, some of which contain meat, while others are completely vegan. It's a popular dish to serve at Ramadan feasts, but it can also be eaten throughout the year.

Sfenj – ال ش ف نج - this quick snack served at street stalls is a type of doughnut cooked in oil. It can be eaten either plain or sprinkled with sugar (or soaked in honey). *Sfenj* are well known throughout the Maghreb region, and traditionally they are sold and eaten either for breakfast in the early morning or as a snack with tea or coffee in the late afternoon.

Orange salad - ال برتقال سلطة - typically eaten at the end of the meal as a light dessert, this simple dish consists of sliced oranges that are drizzled with orange flower water and dusted with cinnamon and either granulated or powdered sugar. Oranges prepared this way are often served with mint tea (see below).

Moroccan mint tea – ال شاي - the Moroccan national drink, it's often referred to as "Berber whiskey" in Morocco. Mint tea is commonly served after a meal, but also at any time throughout the day. The tea is traditionally poured from a special teapot with a long spout that's held high above the glass. This is said to aerate the tea and enhance the flavor as it flows down to the glass.

The tea most commonly used to make mint tea is a Chinese green tea known as gunpowder tea or pearl tea. Fresh mint leaves and sugar are also added. Occasionally honey is used, so if that's the case you can order it sugar-free and then add your own sugar.

Vegan Food in Moroccan Restaurants outside Morocco

You will find many Moroccan restaurants in Europe, and particularly in France, which is home to a large Moroccan community. In my very early days as a vegan, my husband and I took a trip to Normandy over the Christmas holidays. I was still new to vegan travel and was a bit worried about what I would find to eat in northern France, especially on Christmas day when most restaurants would be closed.

My fears of going to bed hungry on Christmas were unfounded, though. We ended up in a Moroccan restaurant in Rouen, where I was served a three-course dinner with a huge helping of vegetarian couscous. The very friendly owner even let me borrow his iPad so I could call my Mom on Skype to wish her a Merry Christmas.

The popularity of Moroccan cuisine is also growing in the United States and in other countries around the world. This is due in large part to the awareness-raising efforts of cookbook authors and chefs like Paula Wolfert and Najat Kaanache, who have done much to promote Moroccan cuisine outside of Morocco.

Restaurants outside the country probably won't have a huge selection of salads like the ones typically served in Morocco, but they will most definitely have plenty of couscous and tajine.

Just about any restaurant will offer a vegetable couscous, and probably a vegetable tajine as well. Some restaurants do cook the vegetables in the same pot as meat, though, so ask about this if it concerns you.

Most restaurants tend to offer just one vegetarian couscous made with an assortment of vegetables. If you grow tired of this and want to try out a different flavor, ask if they'll throw in some dried apricots, prunes, dates, etc. They will most likely have these on hand for use in other, meat-based dishes.

Alternatively, you could ask for some "*tfaya*" (ةيافﺗ) on the side. This thick sauce of raisins and caramelized onions is almost like a jam and adds a delicious sweetness to any couscous dish.

Extra Resources

Marrakech Day Trips is a tour company that offers a number of short day trips to sights in and around Marrakech, as well as longer desert tours lasting for up to four days.

While they are not a vegan company, they understand veganism very well and are able to provide vegan meals on their tours. Some of their tours include mule rides or camel rides, but vegans have the option of walking alongside the animals or riding in the 4x4 to the next bivouac.

Experience it Tours is a US-based tour company that runs tours to Morocco and Tunisia and is also very aware of the needs of vegan travelers. Their Morocco tours last anywhere from 8 to 14 days, and they can match you with a driver who understands how to seek out vegan options when dealing with local hotels and restaurants.

Vegetarian Tagines & Couscous: 60 Delicious Recipes for Moroccan One-Pot Cooking by Ghillie Basan will open your eyes to the huge range of possibilities when it comes to making Morocco's two most popular dishes. Basan's recipes are part of the regular rotation at our house. They sometimes call for *smen* (fermented butter), but this can easily be substituted with oil, and almost all other ingredients are vegan.

Vegetarian Table: North Africa by Kitty Morse is a beautifully illustrated book that comes highly recommended. It includes vegetarian and vegan recipes from all the Maghreb countries, including many from Morocco. Morse was born in Casablanca and has written a number of other Moroccan cookbooks, but not all of them are vegetarian.

Dinners and Dreams is a blog created by Nisrine Merzouki, a Moroccan woman living in the United States. She began the blog back in 2009 as a way to document her family's recipes and reconnect with her origins. She later became vegetarian, and the blog has now morphed into a collection of wholesome, plant-based recipes. You will find recipes for vegan Moroccan dishes as well as other types of food.

moroccan vegan and *moroccan vegans* are two different Facebook groups where you can connect with vegans living in Morocco. Another option is the *Vegans of the Middle East / North Africa* mentioned in the previous chapter.

Chapter Eleven

Thai Cuisine

Vegan Food in Thailand

Thai food is plant-based in many of the same ways that Chinese and other Asian cuisines are: rice serves as the base for most Thai dishes, tofu is a common ingredient, and vegetables are used in abundance. The number of vegan dishes that can be created within this rich and varied cuisine is almost boundless.

As an added bonus, the concept of veganism is well understood in Thai culture, at least in connection with the dietary guidelines followed by many Buddhists. As in Greece, where the easiest way to acquire a vegan meal is by asking for *nistisimo* ("fasting") food, the Thai language also has a magic word that makes it easy to identify and request vegan dishes.

In Thailand, that word is *"jay"*. To let someone know that you follow a vegan diet, you can say *"chan gin jay"* (ฉันกินเจ) if you're female or *"pom gin jay"* (ผมกินเจ) if you're male.

"Jay" food is the food eaten by Buddhist monks and also by some lay Buddhists, especially on particular days of the lunar calendar. *Jay* food is almost always completely vegan. The only caveat is that honey is allowed, and sometimes oyster sauce is also used. Also, in case you're a huge fan of strong-smelling herbs, keep in mind that not just animal products but also onions, garlic and certain pungent herbs are also avoided in *jay* cuisine. But don't worry; this doesn't mean compromising on flavor.

Throughout Thailand, you will come across *jay* restaurants that serve exclusively *jay* food. They are easily identified by signs with the word *"jay"* written in either Thai or Chinese in red letters on a yellow background. In Thai, it's written like this: เจ, and in Chinese, it's written like this: 齋.

The dishes at *jay* restaurants often include many mock meat dishes, so don't be thrown off if you see words like "chicken", "beef" or "pork" on the menu. *Jay* restaurants are often simple shophouse restaurants where the food is prepared ahead of time and is sold until it runs out. This means that opening hours can be erratic, so it's a good idea to arrive early.

The term *"jay"* is of Chinese origin but is pretty widely recognized throughout southern and central Thailand. If you travel to remote regions in the north or northeast of the country, however, there's a chance you may not be understood. In such cases, try using the word "*mangsaweerat*" instead. This is a Thai word that means "vegetarian".

If you are in Thailand in the autumn, you won't want to miss the Nine Emperor Gods Festival, also known as the Vegetarian Festival. This nine-day festival is tied to the lunar calendar, so dates vary, but it usually takes place in October.

For the duration of the festival, many Thai people either abstain from animal products completely or cut way back on their consumption of meat, dairy, and eggs. This creates a large demand for vegan versions of all the usual Thai favorites, so you will have a chance to try all different kinds of dishes that might not be available in vegan versions at other times of the year.

The festival has its origins in both Buddhist and Taoists traditions among the ethnic Chinese population in Thailand. It is most popular in Phuket, where about 35 percent of the population is Thai-Chinese, but it is also celebrated in many other cities. Some restaurants become 100 percent vegan for the duration of the festival, and most will at the very least have a separate vegan menu.

Randi Delano, the creator of the vegan travel blog Veggie Visa and co-creator of the budget travel website Just A Pack, shared with me some of her own experiences traveling as a vegan in Thailand at this time of year:

"The Thailand Vegetarian Festival, or Nine Emperor Gods Festival, takes place every year on the eve of the ninth lunar month of the Chinese calendar. During the nine-day festival, the devout dress in all white and eat "jay" which essentially means vegan.

If you're in Bangkok during this time, you will encounter endless street stalls, restaurants, and even 7/11 shops selling jay food, all advertised with the yellow jay flag.

One would be remiss to skip the main festivities in Bangkok and not make at least one trip to Chinatown. Seemingly endless rows of stalls, all selling vegan food, are neatly lined up next to one another. But this arrangement is the only sense of order you'll experience there.

Between the throngs of crowds and the energetic buzz that feels almost tangible, the atmosphere is, to say the least, chaotic. The only acceptable response, in my opinion, is to seek comfort in as much vegan food as you can possibly fit into your belly, bag, and pockets.

With hundreds of options, this is a completely attainable goal. Be on the lookout for the stand selling peanut brittle for an incredibly lively performance.

Countless options, including dumplings, cakes, and a multitude of unnameable treats you've never seen before make visiting Bangkok during the Vegetarian Festival a dream come true for vegan foodies."

At other times of the year, it's still possible to get great vegan food in mainstream restaurants, and in fact, many of them will have a vegetarian section in their menu. There are, however, certain animal-based ingredients that are used in small amounts in the vast majority of Thai dishes - sometimes even the ones labeled as vegetarian. If you want to avoid animal products completely, you will need to become familiar with the names of these ingredients and get into the habit of asking about them whenever you order food (unless you're in a *jay* restaurant).

The culprits are: fish sauce (น้ำปลา, pronounced "*nam plaa*"), shrimp paste (กะปิ, pronounced "*gapi*"), and oyster sauce (ซอสหอยนางรม, pronounced "*sot hooi naang rom*"). You should assume that fish sauce is in everything, because it usually is. Randi Delano points out that other common sauces and condiments in Thailand might also contain fish sauce:

"Nearly every restaurant in Thailand will have jars of sliced spicy chilies soaking in what I assumed to be soy sauce placed on each table. It was weeks before I learned from an unusually astute waiter that the brown liquid was, in fact, fish sauce."

However, stir-fried dishes and salads are usually made to order on the spot, so you can just ask to replace the fish sauce with soy sauce.

You can also ask to replace any kind of meat with tofu, mushrooms or eggplant. A nice catch-all phrase to get your point across is *"mai gin neua sat"* (ไม่กินเนื้อสัตว์), which means that you would like your dish without any kind of meat.

Curries are a bit trickier, because most restaurants buy pre-made curry pastes from the market, and virtually all of these pastes contain shrimp paste. If you have your heart set on a curry and want to ensure that it doesn't contain shrimp paste, it's best to go to a *jay* restaurant to order it.

In mainstream restaurants, just do the best you can. Accidents will happen and are not worth freaking out about. Remember that we are talking about very small amounts of animal products, so it's important to keep perspective.

The next section lists just a few of the many Thai dishes that are either naturally vegan or can easily be adapted by asking to leave out the fish sauce or other animal-based ingredients.

In addition to the many vegan options available thanks to the traditional Buddhist custom of eating *jay* food, there is also a more Westernized version of veganism that has made its way to Thailand in recent years.

The northern city of Chiang Mai, in particular, has become something of a Mecca for vegan travelers. There you will find a plethora of vegan and vegetarian restaurants serving pizza, burgers and other Western favorites in addition to traditional Thai fare.

Vegan or Veganizable Dishes to Seek Out

Pad Kra Pao - **ผัดกะเพรา** - the better-known version of this dish is *pad kra pao gai,* which is usually translated into English as "Thai basil chicken". The beauty of Thai food, though, is that ingredients are always interchangeable. It's no problem at all to ask for a mushroom version instead by ordering *pad kra pao het* (the word *"het"* in the name of the dish means "mushrooms", and replaces the *"gai",* which means "chicken").

There are three types of basil used in Thai cuisine: Thai sweet basil, lemon basil, and holy basil. The one called for in this dish is holy basil, which has a distinctive, peppery flavor. This type can be difficult to find outside of Thailand, though, so some Thai restaurants in other countries will cheat by using Thai sweet basil instead. Another variation of this dish uses eggplant as the main ingredient rather than mushrooms and is called *pad makua yow*. Note that the eggplants in Thailand are long and green. They are quite different in appearance from the fat, dark purple ones found in Europe and North America, but the taste is similar.

Tom Yum - ต้มยำ - Tom yum is a popular spicy and sour soup flavored with lemongrass, galangal, and kaffir lime leaves. It's often made with some kind of meat, but if you want it with just vegetables you can add the words "*pak ruam*" (vegetables) at the end. Alternatively, you could also order it with mushrooms instead of vegetables by asking for "*tom yum het*". Note that the lemongrass and galangal are not meant to be eaten, even though they are usually left in the soup when serving to impart extra flavor. The kaffir lime leaves are technically edible, but most people eat around those too. Tom yum can be served on its own or with rice.

Tom Kha Taohu - ต้มข่าเต้าหู้ - this spicy and sour coconut soup is popular in both Thai and Lao cuisines. The main difference between the two is that, while the Lao version calls for dill weed, in Thailand cilantro is used instead. *Tom kha* is most commonly made with chicken, in which case it's called *tom kha gai*, but you can ask for it with tofu (*taohu*) instead. Another veganizable variation is the one made with mushrooms, which is called *tom kha het*. Like *tom yum*, this soup is also flavored with lemongrass, galangal, and kaffir lime leaves, but the addition of coconut milk adds a whole new dimension to the flavor profile.

Pad Pak Ruam Mit - ผัดผักรวมมิตร - this is a simple and healthy dish of stir-fried mixed vegetables, typically served over white rice. The words "ruam mit" mean "everything mixed together", so the cook will probably just use whatever vegetables are in season and on hand. Typical ingredients include snow peas, broccoli, carrots, cabbage, cauliflower, mushrooms, bok choy and bean sprouts.

Som Tam - ส้มตำ - this cold salad dish originated in the Isan region in the northeast of Thailand, near the border with Laos. The main ingredient is shredded green papaya, which is simply a papaya that has been picked when it is unripe and still hard and green. Unripe papayas have a completely different texture and flavor from the ripe, orange fruit; rather than being soft and sweet, they are crisp, firm and tangy. Other key ingredients in the salad are roasted peanuts, sour lime juice, and palm sugar. There are several variations of the dish, each of which has a different name and contains different non-vegan ingredients like dried shrimp, salted crab, or freshwater snails. But since it's made to order on the spot, you can tell the vendor you don't want any of that.

Soup Nor Mai - ซุบหน่อไม้ - Don't let the word "soup" in the name fool you. This is a transliteration of the Thai name, not a translation into English. This dish is most definitely not a soup; it could best be described as a spicy bamboo shoot salad. Sliced bamboo shoots are boiled and mixed with onions, chili powder, cilantro and other herbs to create this flavorful dish.

Pad Thai - ผัดไทย - the name of this famous stir-fried noodle dish literally means "stir-fried Thai style", and it is most commonly served at street food stalls or at very casual, inexpensive restaurants in Thailand. It is one of Thailand's national dishes and is probably the dish that foreigners are the most familiar with. Ingredients can vary, but it always starts with a base of rice noodles and is flavored with lime, chili pepper, and tamarind pulp and topped with crushed peanuts and bean sprouts. It's also usually served with a lime wedge on the side. The non-vegan ingredients to avoid are shrimp, eggs, and of course fish sauce. Some cooks also add different types of meat, so just ask for yours to be "*jay*" to cover all your bases.

***Khanom Krok* - ขนมครก** - these miniature round pancakes made from coconut milk and rice flour are a long-standing feature of Thai street food. From a distance, you might mistake them for poached eggs, but *khanom krok* are completely vegan. They are made in a special cast-iron frying pan with indentations in it. The two sides of the pancake are cooked separately and then stuck together to create the finished product.

Khanom krok can come with a variety of different toppings or fillings, some are savory and others are sweet. Examples include sweetcorn, taro, grated coconut, and even shitake mushroom. They are sold from street stalls in the afternoon, and later in the evening at night markets.

***Khao Lam* - ข้าวหลาม** - the most distinctive characteristic of this street food snack is the way it is prepared. The word "*khao*" means "sticky rice" in Thai, while "*lam*" refers to the cooking process. Sticky rice is a particular variety of rice that grows mainly in Southeast and East Asia and is especially sticky when cooked. It is sometimes also referred to as "glutinous rice" in English. Don't let that name fool you, though. Like all other varieties of rice, glutinous rice is gluten free.

To make *khao lam*, a mixture of sticky rice, sugar, coconut milk and red beans is roasted inside a bamboo tube. The part of the mixture that is exposed to the flame at the end of the tube is allowed to caramelize. This sweet treat is sold at street food stalls and is also traditionally given to monks by devotees wishing to earn merit.

Khao Niao Mamuang - ข้าวเหนียวมะม่วง - known in English as "mango sticky rice", this traditional Thai dish consists of sticky rice that is seasoned with coconut milk and served with fresh slices of ripe mango. It can be eaten with a fork, a spoon, or even with the hands, and it can be served either warm or at room temperature. In Thailand, it's most often eaten in April or May, when mangoes are in season. Mango sticky rice is probably the most well-known Thai sweet among foreign tourists in Thailand, but there are also a number of other traditional Thai sweets made with sticky rice.

Vegan Food in Thai Restaurants outside Thailand

The international popularity of Thai cuisine is a relatively recent phenomenon. As a result, the dishes served in Thai restaurants outside of Thailand have remained fairly authentic thus far and are primarily ones that are also popular in Thailand.

The main difference is that some Thai restaurants abroad may substitute hard-to-find ingredients with others that are more widely available locally. For example, in Western countries, the basil used in *pad kra pao* might be Thai sweet basil instead of the harder-to-find holy basil.

While these kinds of substitutions will change the flavor of the dish to some extent, vegan ingredients are generally substituted with other vegan ingredients and vice versa. This means that the advice given in the previous sections on ordering vegan food applies both inside and outside of Thailand.

Of course, if your server is not Thai then they probably won't understand you if you use the word "*jay*" to explain what you do and don't eat. In that case, just explain it as you would in any other restaurant.

As for what to order, spring or summer rolls are good starter options, as is green papaya salad. When it comes to the main dish, you can ask to replace any meat with tofu, or just leave it out altogether. Many Thai restaurants will have a separate vegetarian section of the menu. It's still a good idea to ask about fish sauce and shrimp paste, however, as these are often added even to the vegetarian dishes.

If you order noodle dishes, just ask for rice noodles instead of the yellow wheat noodles, which probably contain egg. *Pad thai* is always served with rice noodles anyway and is a delicious vegan option; just be sure to specify no shrimp, eggs or fish sauce.

Although sweets are popular as snacks in Thailand, there is no custom of ending the meal with something sweet. Thai restaurants in Western countries, however, have adapted to local customs by creating a dessert menu of traditional sweet dishes. And since dairy products are hardly used at all in Thai cuisine, the dessert section of the menu usually includes some vegan options. Two common examples are banana fritters and the perennial favorite - mango sticky rice.

Extra Resources

May Kaidee's Thai Vegetarian and Vegan Cookbook by vegetarian restaurateur and cooking instructor May Kaidee. The author owns a chain of vegetarian restaurants in Thailand, Cambodia, and New York City that serve delicious vegetarian and vegan Thai food at reasonable prices. Cooking classes are also offered at the restaurant locations in Bangkok and Chiang Mai. I was first introduced to May Kaidee's restaurant in 2007, when it was recommended to me by a friend who had lived in Bangkok. I went there for a meal and loved it, and I even got to meet the famous May

Kaidee herself! My signed copy of this cookbook gets used frequently in our house. I love the Pad Thai recipe.

The Best of Vegetarian Thai Food by Sisamon Kongpan is another cookbook of vegetarian Thai recipes that comes highly recommended.

Eating Thai Food is a blog written by Mark Wiens. While Mark is not vegan or vegetarian, he did complete a one-month vegetarian challenge while living in Bangkok, and during that time he wrote every day about all the different vegetarian dishes he ate there. Those daily blog posts are a great source of info on the types of veggie foods available in Thailand.

Vegan Food Quest is a blog written by vegan couple Paul and Caryl Eyers, who have traveled extensively throughout Southeast Asia and are currently based in Cambodia. Their blog includes restaurant reviews of a number of different restaurants in Thailand, as well as vegan destination guides covering Bangkok, Chiang Mai, and Koh Kood.

There are a number of Facebook groups for vegans living in Thailand, the largest of which are *Vegan of Thailand* and *Vegan Thailand*.

Chapter Twelve

Vietnamese Cuisine

Vegan Food in Vietnamese Restaurants

Like China and Thailand, Vietnam also has a long Buddhist tradition that has deeply influenced the national cuisine. Buddhist restaurants like those in Thailand are found in even greater abundance in Vietnam and are frequented by many locals. In Vietnam, these Buddhist eateries are known as *chay* restaurants. These are then further categorized into different types of *chay* restaurants, but we'll get to that in a minute.

They serve veganized versions of all the most famous national Vietnamese dishes, as well as many unique regional and local specialties. From "white rose" dumplings in Hoi An to the spicy noodle soup called "*bún bò*" that the city of Huế is famous for, you will be able to sample vegan renditions of just about any local dish you can imagine.

Unfortunately, most foreign visitors to the country don't know about these restaurants, which is a real shame. This chapter will focus mainly on bringing you up to speed with Vietnamese Buddhist customs as they relate to vegan eating, because knowing about these customs will make it so much easier for you to uncover the abundance of vegan food available in Vietnam.

Many Vietnamese Buddhists follow a vegan diet either on a permanent basis, which is known as "*trường chay*" in Vietnamese, or on particular dates, which is known as "*kỳ chay*". Those who are *kỳ chay* eat vegan on specific days of the lunar calendar. You can think of this as a Vietnamese version of meatless Mondays.

Some people who follow this practice view it as a transition to a fully vegan lifestyle, while others do it to earn merit but don't intend to become fully vegan. Buddhists who follow the *kỳ chay* schedule will, at a minimum, eat vegan on the 1st and 15th days of the lunar calendar. In addition, some will also eat vegan on the 8th, 14th, 23rd, 29th, and 30th days of the lunar calendar.

On these days, Buddhist restaurants are particularly busy, so it's a good idea to arrive early. In fact, *chay* restaurants get so packed with customers at these times that many of them close the following day to give their staff a much-needed break. So, on the 2nd and 16th days of the lunar calendar, you may need to look elsewhere for your meals.

186

This is not a problem, as plenty of mainstream restaurants also have vegan dishes, or even an entire vegan/vegetarian section of the menu, and there are also many Vietnamese street food snacks that are naturally vegan. You just might want to ask a few questions about hidden ingredients like fish sauce, shrimp paste, and meat broth.

But if you want to enjoy an abundance of vegan options, including vegan versions of dishes that normally contain animal products, then you'll definitely want to seek out some Buddhist *chay* restaurants.

So, how do you find these vegan havens? Some of them are listed on *HappyCow*, but here's another great shortcut suggested by the very helpful website *Vegan Vietnam*:

On Google maps, look for pagodas (temples), which are marked with an icon in the shape of a wheel. Then look at the eateries nearby. You are bound to find some with names that begin with "*nhà hàng chay*", "*quán chay*" or "*cơm chay*". All of these are vegetarian/vegan eateries. You can also just do a direct search for these phrases followed by the name of the city you're in.

While all of these places serve vegan food, there are some differences between them. *Quán chay* and *cơm chay* restaurants are small, informal eateries that serve simple meals and tend to have a limited menu. The choices here consist mainly of rice and veggie dishes and/or noodle soups.

At these eateries, prices are cheap, but the service is basic, and opening hours can be erratic. As a side note, many businesses in Vietnam close for a couple of hours after lunch, so you may have a hard time finding anything open between 2 p.m. and 4 p.m.

Nhà hàng chay differ from *quán chay* and *cơm chay* in that they are mid-range restaurants with fixed hours and more sophisticated décor. Think tablecloths and matching sets of wooden chairs, as opposed to brightly-colored plastic stools.

They are guaranteed to have a wide choice of vegan dishes, and many of them are 100 percent vegan. However, you may see some menu items that contain eggs, and also drinks that contain milk (dairy products are not typically part of Vietnamese cooking, so aside from the drinks menu you don't need to worry about them).

Even though the generally accepted meaning of *chay* in the Buddhist sense does not include any animal products, some *chay* restaurants seem to take a few liberties with this, so just be aware that you might occasionally come across eggs and dairy in these places.

The word *"chay"* is also useful when ordering food in mainstream restaurants, as it can be used to indicate a vegetarian/vegan version of a particular dish. For example, if you want a vegan bowl of phở – the noodle soup for which Vietnam is famous – ask for "phở chay". Similarly, asking for a "bánh mì chay" will get you a bánh mì sandwich filled with mock meat or tofu.

Mainstream restaurants will often have several vegan dishes anyway, but be aware that the phrases "vegetarian dishes" and "vegetable dishes" are sometimes confused when translating menus into English.

This means that you might come across some dishes that predominantly feature vegetables but that do also contain bits of meat. This is another case where asking for a *"chay"* version of the dish comes in handy. *Chay* is your magic word in Vietnam. If the section of the menu is called *món chay* in Vietnamese, then you can rest assured that the dishes are vegetarian (and probably vegan).

Many national dishes can easily be veganized, including hotpot and clay pot dishes made with tofu, mushrooms, eggplant or any other vegetables. Eggplant is actually quite abundant in Vietnam and is cooked in a number of different ways.

Vegan or Veganizable Dishes to Seek Out

Cơm Gà Chay - the words "*cơm*" and "*gà*" literally mean "rice" and "chicken" respectively, and this dish of shredded chicken, yellow rice, fresh herbs and chili paste is popular throughout Vietnam and elsewhere in Southeast Asia. Vegan versions are widely available in *chay* restaurants. Each place has its own secret recipe, so you may find chicken made from tofu, mushrooms, or flour.

Phở - probably the most famous Vietnamese dish, phở is a noodle soup made with broth, rice noodles and other ingredients. It's a popular street food throughout the country, and regional varieties may vary with regard to the size of the noodles, the sweetness of the broth, and the choice of herbs used. While most phở in mainstream restaurants is not vegan, it's a very common offering in the country's many vegetarian restaurants.

Bánh Xèo - the name of this dish means "sizzling pancake", and indeed, this savory pancake is best enjoyed when it's straight out of the pan and still sizzling. The yellow hue might trick you into thinking it's an omelet, but actually, that golden color comes from turmeric, which is mixed with rice flour and coconut milk to make the batter. *Bánh xèo* are stuffed with various fillings, and common vegan fillings include bean sprouts, tofu, and mushrooms. In some parts of

Vietnam, they are then rolled up in lettuce or other greens and made into the shape of a spring roll.

Bánh Mì Chay - a sandwich made with a French baguette that is stuffed with veggies, mock meats, and/or tofu. This fusion dish is a product of French colonialism, as it was the French who introduced the baguette to Vietnam. Ironically, the *bánh mì* has since become the most famous form of Vietnamese street food and is now popular in France and many other countries around the world.

In Vietnam, you can try looking around Buddhist temples for a fully vegan *bánh mì* cart. If that doesn't work, then just go to a regular *bánh mì* vendor and ask them to replace the meat (*không thịt*) with veggies (*nhiều rau*). Just watch it being made to be sure they don't add any paté, eggs or other non-vegan ingredients.

Gỏi Cuốn - these fresh spring rolls (also known as summer rolls) can be made with fresh vegetables, rice vermicelli, sprouts or even tofu, which is then rolled up inside a sheet of rice paper. They are served cold or at room temperature and are not fried or cooked on the outside. In southern Vietnam, they are called "*gỏi cuốn*", which means "salad rolls", whereas in the north they are known as "*nem cuốn*".

Gỏi Bắp Chuối - "Gỏi" is a generic term in Vietnamese for any type of salad (remember the name for the "salad rolls" we just learned about?), but these salads are a bit different from the ones you may be used to. For one, they usually don't contain any lettuce. Instead, the base of the salad could be any number of vegetables, fruits or roots.

Gỏi bắp chuối is a popular salad made with sliced banana flowers, which are the large, purple flowers on a banana tree. These flowers have a crunchy, almost meaty texture. They are combined with various vegetables, herbs, and pickles for a tasty and healthy meal.

Cháo - this thick rice porridge, usually referred to as "congee" in English, can be anything from a simple breakfast food to a hearty main dish, depending on what toppings are added to it. *Cháo* has humble origins among low-income families, who use it to make their rice rations stretch further.

It is believed to be both fortifying and easy to digest, and for these reasons the Vietnamese will often turn to it as comfort food, especially when they're feeling under the weather. Common vegan toppings include mushrooms, fresh herbs, and ginger.

Lẩu - this "hot pot" is a spicy variation of the Vietnamese sour soup (*canh chua*), and the elaborate way in which it's served is almost a theatrical production. First, you will be presented with some plain noodles, leafy greens, and sauce. Your waiter will then bring a portable hot pot cooker right to your table.

The contents of the pot will depend on the type of *lẩu* but may include mushrooms, kimchi, vegetables, tofu or other goodies floating in broth. The pot will be placed on top of the cooker and left there to bubble away.

Once the mixture is sufficiently hot, you can add the leafy greens and then pour the hot soup over your noodles. Lẩu is most often enjoyed by a group of friends as a communal meal.

Mì Quảng - Quảng-style noodles ("mì" means "noodles are fat rice noodles that are cooked with turmeric and topped with peanuts. In the south of Vietnam, this dish is served as a soup, whereas in central Vietnam, where the dish originates, it's made with just enough broth to wet the noodles and no more.

Served alongside the noodles are toasted Vietnamese sesame rice crackers, fried shallots, and various herbs. It is one of the most popular dishes in Vietnam and is eaten both at major celebrations and as an everyday lunch.

Tàu Hủ Nước Đường - this extremely soft tofu is sometimes called "tofu pudding" in English and is popular throughout Asia. In Vietnam, it's served different ways, depending on the region. In the north, you'll find it served with sugar and chia seeds, while in central Vietnam it's cooked with spicy ginger, and in the south, it's served warm with lychee and coconut water.

This sweet dish is often eaten for breakfast at street food stalls, and you can also find a packaged version of it in supermarkets.

Nước Rau Má - whether you're looking for a thirst quencher or a vitamin boost, a tall glass of pennywort (*rau má*) juice is sure to do the trick. This green herb has numerous health benefits, from improving eyesight to relieving arthritis pain. Fresh pennywort juice is available from juice stalls on the street, and also at restaurants. Sugar is optional, but most people choose to add some to take away the tartness of the drink.

Vegan Food in Vietnamese Restaurants outside Vietnam

Vietnamese food hasn't quite reached all corners of the globe yet, although its popularity around the world is growing at a rapid pace. Considering how quickly Thai cuisine has taken

194

the world by storm in just a few short decades, you can expect Vietnamese cuisine to follow close behind on the international food scene.

In this increasingly globalized world, it's only a matter of time before this delicious and healthy cuisine will be served in cities of all sizes on every inhabited continent (Antarctica might have to wait awhile).

In the meantime, there are many Vietnamese restaurants in larger cities like Paris, London, and Berlin, and some of these restaurants are even fully vegetarian. If you do find yourself in close proximity to a Vietnamese restaurant, don't pass up the chance to taste the delicious flavors of the unique herbs, spices, and vegetables found in Vietnam.

If you are dining in a mainstream Vietnamese restaurant that's not fully vegetarian, they will often have a separate vegetarian section of the menu. Here you will find rice and noodle dishes with various combinations of vegetables and tofu.

Even if there is no vegetarian section, there are bound to be a few vegan items that are part of the regular menu, such as spring or summer rolls. The kitchen is guaranteed to have lots of fresh vegetables on hand, too, so don't hesitate to ask for a plate of mixed vegetables with rice or noodles.

This is often much more exciting than it sounds, and you may discover some vegetables you've never encountered before.

While proper restaurants offering a large choice of Vietnamese dishes may still be relatively few on the ground, one Vietnamese specialty that has really caught on in recent years is the *bánh mì*.

If you come across a sandwich shop serving up *bánh mì*, ask the staff to make a vegan version with tofu and/or vegetables. It just might be the best sandwich you've ever eaten.

Extra Resources

The Viet Vegan - If you want to make some scrumptious Vietnamese food yourself, then Lisa Le, a.k.a. The Viet Vegan, is a good person to learn from. Lisa, a twenty-something Canadian-born Vietnamese woman, shares lots of different types of recipes on her blog, including some Vietnamese ones. When she began the blog she was lacto-ovo vegetarian, but she then became vegan in October 2013 and has been posting all vegan recipes ever since. She also has a fun YouTube channel with lots of recipe videos.

Vegan Vietnam - This website is quite new but has already established itself as a fantastic source of information about where to find delicious vegan food in Vietnam. It includes destination guides to specific towns and cities, as well as more general cultural tips.

Vegan Food Quest - Caryl and Paul Eyers are a couple of vegan food lovers who left their home in England in January 2014 to go traveling the globe on a mission to find, eat and write about the best vegan food in the world. Since then they have spent most of their time in Southeast Asia, including lots of travels in Vietnam. Their website includes vegan destination guides for Ho Chi Minh City, Hội An, Côn Đảo and Nha Trang.

Karma Waters is a vegan restaurant with branches in Hoi An and Danang, and they also run one-day vegan tours that include a homestay on the Cham Islands and an organic vegetable village tour.

Lịch Việt Nam (for iPhone) and *Lịch Việt* (for Android). If you want to keep track of what day it is on the lunar calendar (so you'll know whether the local *chay* restaurants will be packed with locals or closed for the day), these two Vietnamese calendar apps can help you do that. They are in Vietnamese but are not too difficult to navigate.

Vegan Vietnam is a Facebook group that is moderated by Caryl and Paul Eyers - the couple behind Vegan Food Quest. Posts here are mostly in English, whereas in the group *Vegan Vietnam - Cộng Đồng Ăn Chay* most posts are written in Vietnamese.

Conclusion

I hope that this book has opened your eyes to the abundance of delicious, vegan food the world has to offer. The dishes I talked about in the pages of this book are definitely not the only vegan dishes in these 11 cuisines. In fact, each chapter could easily have been expanded into a full-length book of its own.

In the future, I do plan to publish vegan guides to individual world cuisines, starting with Italian. My next book, *Italy for Veggie Lovers*, will be released in 2018. You can download the first chapter for free at thenomadicvegan/veganitaly.

Keep in mind also that the cuisines discussed in this book are certainly not the only ones that have delicious vegan food to offer. The reason I chose these particular cuisines is because they are widely available. I wanted you to know that no matter where you are, you can walk into a restaurant serving one of these cuisines and order a healthy and satisfying vegan meal.

But even cuisines that have a reputation for being extraordinarily difficult for vegans and vegetarians still have plenty of surprises in store if you dig deep enough, and if you go into the experience with an abundance mindset.

Spain, for example, has gazpacho, vegetable paella, and a huge selection of vegan tapas. Even France has vegan specialties like *socca* - a savory pancake made from chickpea flour that is hugely popular in Nice, Marseilles, and other cities and towns in the south.

Regardless of where you're headed - even if it's just down the street to your local Chinese restaurant - it's time for you to put your new-found knowledge to good use and become a veggieplaneteer! I challenge you to use this book as a jumping-off point for making many new discoveries, whether they be discoveries of new foods, new cultures, or even a new you. And I want to hear about what you discover!

So here's your homefun assignment (it's like homework, except that it's fun!): eat a vegan dish or food that you've never tasted before. It could be one of the dishes described in this book or one that you discover on your own. It could even be one that you make yourself! Then post a photo of your vegan discovery on Twitter, Facebook or Instagram with the hashtag #veggieplaneteer.

I'll be looking out for your photo, and I may even share it with my own followers! I can't wait to see what you discover.

On the following pages, you will find a list of resources to guide you as you take your next steps on this journey. I've also created a special page on my website with links to ALL of these resources in one handy place. You can find all the links at:

thenomadicvegan.com/resources

I have included all of the resources mentioned throughout the book as well as some additional resources that are useful for vegan travel in general, including for trips to places other than the countries discussed in this book. Happy travels on this beautiful Veggie Planet!

Extra Resources

Developing an Abundance Mindset

Headspace. A guided meditation app

MS Word Journal Templates. For creating your own DIY gratitude journal

The Five Minute Journal. A popular hardcover gratitude journal

Thnx4. A free, online gratitude journal

Affirmations. Suggested affirmations focusing on gratitude and food, for use in your daily practice.

The Vegan Lifestyle

If you are new to the vegan lifestyle and would like to learn more about the reasons for and the benefits of choosing plant-based foods over animal-based ones, here are the top educational resources I recommend:

Films

Cowspiracy: The Sustainability Secret is a groundbreaking environmental documentary that uncovers the most destructive industry facing the planet today.

Forks over Knives examines the profound claim that most, if not all, of the degenerative diseases that afflict us can be controlled, or even reversed, by rejecting animal-based and processed foods.

What the Health is the groundbreaking follow-up film from the creators of the award-winning documentary Cowspiracy. It uncovers the secret to preventing and even reversing chronic diseases – and investigates why the nation's leading health organizations don't want us to know about it.

Earthlings is a documentary film about humankind's total dependence on animals for economic purposes. Presented in five chapters (pets, food, clothing, entertainment and scientific research), the film is narrated by Joaquin Phoenix and features music by Moby.

Books

Eating Animals by Jonathan Safran Foer is a very thorough book examining animal agribusiness that reveals the ethical implications of factory farming.

The World Peace Diet by Will Tuttle presents the outlines of a more empowering understanding of our world, based on the comprehending the far-reaching implications of our food choices.

Why We Love Dogs, Eat Pigs and Wear Cows by Melanie Joy offers an absorbing look at why and how humans can so wholeheartedly devote ourselves to certain animals and then allow others to suffer needlessly, especially those slaughtered for our consumption.

The 30-Day Vegan Challenge by Colleen Patrick-Goudreau holds your hand every step of the way as you try out the vegan lifestyle for 30 days, giving you the tools, resources, and recipes you need to make the vegan transition.

The Plant-Based Journey by Lani Muelrath offers a positive, non-judgmental approach and provides the support you need to make your transition into eating plant-based a fun and (ful)filling experience.

Isa Does It by Isa Chandra Moskowitz is my go-to recipe book. It includes recipes, tips, and strategies for easy, delicious vegan meals every day of the week, from America's bestselling vegan cookbook author.

Podcasts

Food for Thought has been running for more than 10 years. This podcast by Colleen Patrick Goudreau covers all aspects of living healthfully and compassionately.

Main Street Vegan is hosted by Victoria Moran, who interviews vegans from all walks of life who are doing exciting things to grow the vegan movement.

The Bearded Vegans moves beyond the basic Vegan 101 and creates more nuanced discussions for the seasoned vegan.

Vegan Warrior Princesses Attack is a podcast with in-depth, unapologetic discussions of vegan issues by two modern day vegan warrior princesses, Callie and Nichole.

The Brownble Podcast teaches you how to cook the foods you love, vegan style, gives you tons of inspiration for your daily meals, supports on your vegan journey, and helps you make peace with food and improve your relationship with it.

YouTubers

ModVegan posts videos discussing animal rights, minimalism, sustainability, futurism and technology. The channel was born out of a desire to redesign vegan living for a new era and explore how veganism can move forward.

Bite Size Vegan is veganism simplified. The host, Emily, delivers vegan education in the form of "vegan nugget" videos with loads of information distilled down to fast, power-packed bites.

A Privileged Vegan is hosted by Marine, who makes videos about pro-intersectional justice, always making sure that humans and other animals are a part of that conversation.

The Lost Lemurian is a channel by Karyn Jane, who makes videos about veganism, spirituality, travel, environmentalism, and a zero waste lifestyle. She aims to help the world become a kinder place, and her motto is, "Just be kind; it's not hard".

Brownble also has a YouTube channel in addition to their podcast, blog and membership program. On the channel, you'll find Vegan cooking and lifestyle tips, vegan recipes and all the support you need on your plant-based journey.

Plant Based Bride is a channel hosted by Elizabeth Turnbull, a young Canadian woman who makes videos about veganism, minimalism, and vegan and cruelty-free beauty.

Vegan Travel Worldwide

The Vegan Passport. This handy smartphone app includes a full explanation in 79 languages of what vegans do and do not eat. It's also available as a paperback phrasebook that can be ordered from the Vegan Society website.

HappyCow App. Search for vegan, vegetarian and vegan-friendly restaurants in your destination with this very useful app (or on the HappyCow website). You can use the app to research your destination in advance using the "Trip" feature, or just see the options nearest you once you arrive. You can also contribute to the directory by adding new restaurants you discover or reviewing the ones already listed.

Vegan Xpress App lists all the vegan items available at many American chain restaurants and fast food outlets. If you're traveling in the United States, it's very helpful. In addition to the menu guide, there's also a food guide that lists accidentally vegan candies, cookies and other snack foods available in grocery stores, convenience stores, gas stations, etc.

Green Earth Travel. This travel agency run by longtime vegan and seasoned world traveler Donna Zeigfinger focuses on vegan, vegetarian and eco-travel. The agency specializes in organizing individualized excursions, including volunteer vacation packages and adventure travel trips that leave a light footprint on the earth.

Veg Jaunts and Journeys organizes activity-packed, reasonably-priced vegan group tours to destinations in the United States and Europe. Some of the tours are timed to coincide with vegan festivals, such as Vegan Summerfest in Berlin. In 2018, I will be personally leading their tours to Italy and Portugal.

Vegan Travel Club offers vegan tours to destinations that include southern Italy, New York City, and Peru. The tours are accompanied by well-known vegan chefs, bloggers, and activists, such as Matt Frazier of No Meat Athlete and Julieanna Hever, aka the Plant-Based Dietitian.

VegVoyages organizes off-the-beaten-path vegan adventure tours in Asian destinations, including India, Malaysia, Thailand, Laos, and Indonesia. Tour participants have the chance to taste unique regional and local home-cooked dishes that are not typically found on restaurant menus.

Bravietour. This vegan-run tour company in Brazil offers a sustainable vegan food trip to Rio de Janeiro and the surrounding areas. In addition to fully vegan meals, the trip also includes visits to local community gardens and animal protection projects.

Blissed Out Retreats is run by vegan chef and yoga teacher Christy Morgan, who offers retreats around the world that are packed full of love and fun, cultural experiences, movement & educational activities, and gourmet plant-based meals, with plenty of free time to recharge.

Vegan Food Tours offers culinary day tours in London, Barcelona and Amsterdam that focus on vegan versions of the authentic cuisine of each city. From rich and creamy Dutch pralines in Amsterdam to a full English breakfast in London to paella in Barcelona, this is the perfect way to show your friends and family that vegan food is much more than carrot sticks and lettuce. Veggie Planet readers can get a 10% discount on any tour by using the promo code GOVEGAN2017.

The Essential Vegan Travel Guide by Caitlin Galer-Unti is a useful book that shows you how to research and locate vegan-friendly (or vegetarian, raw, or gluten-free) fare in any city. Beyond the food, the book offers hints for connecting with local vegans, choosing a place to stay, packing, and traveling (and keeping the peace) with non-vegan companions.

Vegan Trip Planner. Cailin Galer-Unti, author of *The Essential Vegan Travel Guide*, also offers a vegan trip planning service where she creates a customized dining itinerary for your trip. Each itinerary contains vegan-friendly eating options that are near your accommodation and the major attractions, as well as activities and vegan events, all laid out on a handy downloadable map.

Epic Animal Quest is a social enterprise run by a world-traveling family that works with animal shelters and sanctuaries around the world to directly help the animals and raise awareness. If you want to know about vegan family travel, they have lots of info to share.

Veggie Hotels lists vegetarian and vegan hotels, B&Bs and guesthouses in more than 60 countries worldwide. Check their special offers for deals on yoga retreats, vegan cooking courses, and other events.

Vegan Hotels is a smaller website that focuses exclusively on hotels and other types of accommodation where all the food on offer is vegan. The website also features recipes from top vegan chefs working at some of the hotels and resorts features on the site.

Vegan Travel is a non-profit community-run site where vegans can come together from around the world to share their passion for travel and adventure. Anyone can join the community and ask questions in the forums, review restaurants, and upload blog posts about their own vegan travels.

Vegan Platform is a new online marketplace where you can order plant-based dishes from home cooks, catering companies, and restaurants, whether you're traveling or sitting on the couch. The platform is just getting started, but once more food sellers join it could be really useful.

AirBnB is a community marketplace where people can list, discover and book unique accommodations around the world.

There are many benefits to staying in an apartment or other local accommodation rather than a hotel when traveling.

One is that you'll have access to a kitchen, so if you're tired of eating out at every meal, or just want to save money, you can cook for yourself. If you create an account with the link at nomadicvegan.com/airbnb you will get a $40 credit towards your first stay.

Vegvisits is basically a veggie version of AirBnB. The database is much smaller, but the advantage is that you can book accommodation with a vegetarian or vegan host who can offer local insight into the vegan scene, or even just rent out their kitchen for a few hours if you want to prepare your own food. And if you just can't get going in the morning without a green smoothie, you can even narrow your search according to the kitchen appliances available and search for a place with a blender!

Kindred Spirits is a directory that connects vegans and vegetarians who are interested in house sitting or house swapping.

House sitting can be a great way to save on accommodation costs while traveling. In many cases, house sitting duties also involve pet sitting, so this option is best for people who like to be around animals.

Todo Vegano. This bilingual (English and Spanish) website contains a directory of vegan and vegan-friendly places to eat throughout all of Latin America. It also lists events, such as vegan cooking classes.

Libby and Marcel (formerly *Eat Away*) are a vegan couple traveling the world. They post beautiful videos on their YouTube channel, including many that highlight local vegan foods.

China and Chinese Food

ChinesePod. A language learning podcast and website with lots of great learning tools, including a video course on Chinese pronunciation.

The Chinese Vegan Kitchen. A cookbook by Donna Klein with more than 225 easy but authentic vegan Chinese recipes you can prepare in your own kitchen.

China Sichuan Food. A recipe blog by Elaine Luo, who grew up in Sichuan and shares recipes from all over China. Vegan recipes are tagged for easy reference.

The China Study. A bestselling book by T. Colin Campbell, Ph.D, that explains in layman's terms the results of the most comprehensive nutrition study ever conducted.

The Hutong. A culture exchange center in Beijing that offers culinary market tours and cooking classes, many of which are vegan-friendly.

Ethiopia and Ethiopian Food

A Teff Love: Adventures in Vegan Ethiopian Cooking. A cookbook of vegan Ethiopian recipes by Kittee Berns.

Mesob Across America: Ethiopian Food in the U.S.A. A book written by Harry Kloman that takes an in-depth look at the history and culture of food in Ethiopia and also explores how Ethiopian restaurants emerged in the US. Kloman also keeps a blog on Ethiopian food.

Emahoy Hannah's Facebook page. A page run by an Ethiopian nun who lives in a monastery in southern Florida maintains an updated list of the fasting dates each year.

Greece and Greek Food

The Greek Vegan. A recipe website run by Kiki Vagianos, who also produces Nisteia Magazine, which features authentic, traditional Greek vegan recipes.

Yasou: A Magical Fusion of Greek & Middle Eastern Vegan Cuisine. A recipe book by Miriam Sorrell, who has Greek, Turkish, and Maltese origins.

Bamboo Vegan. An all-vegan shop in the center of Athens that sells a wide range of vegan cooking ingredients and packaged, ready-to-eat foods, as well as fresh baked goods. They also have an online shop.

Vegan Life Festival. The first vegan festival held in Greece, in November 2016. Also check their Facebook page to find out about upcoming events.

Turkey and Turkish Food

Culinary Backstreets. A tour company that offers culinary walks in about a dozen cities around the world. On request, they can offer a completely vegan version of their tour through Istanbul's historic district of Beyoğlu.

Ahara Vegan and Yoga Hotel. The first 100 percent vegan hotel on the Turkish Riviera, located in Kizilot.

Kartepe Farm Animal Sanctuary. An animal sanctuary located about 100 kilometers from Istanbul where visitors and volunteers are welcome. Also in Kartepe is the

Raw Gourmets International Culinary Arts and Hospitality Institute. A cooking school run by Turkey's top raw chef, Mehmet Ak. The Institute teaches classes and workshops and also offers accommodation.

The Turkish Vegan and Vegetarian Association. Their website is only in Turkish, but you can email them at tvd@tvd.org. to find out about local vegan events.

India and Indian Food

Veg Voyages. A vegan tour company that runs a number of different vegan tours to India, ranging in length from 8 to 16 days.

Veggie Hotels. A hotel directory that lists more than 70 hotels, resorts, and other accommodation options in India that serve only vegetarian food in their restaurants. Those that have been recommended as being particularly vegan-friendly include Shreyas Retreat in Bangalore, Erandia Marari Ayurveda Beach Resort in Kerala, and Kairali Ayurvedic Healing Village, also in Kerala.

Holy Cow! Vegan Recipes. A recipe blog by Vaishali, who is of Indian origin and lives in Washington, D.C. The blog includes more than 800 vegan recipes, both Indian and from other cuisines.

Vegan Richa's Indian Kitchen. A recipe book by popular vegan blogger and recipe developer Richa Hingle.

The Indian Vegan Kitchen: More Than 150 Quick and Healthy Homestyle Recipes. A cookbook by renowned nutritionist and cooking instructor Madhu Gadia. The book contains no photos, but lots of recipes.

Vegan Indian Cooking: 140 Simple and Healthy Vegan Recipes. A recipe book by Anupy Singla. This one has fewer recipes than Gadia's but is illustrated with color photographs throughout.

Italy and Italian Food

Italy for Veggie Lovers. My upcoming book showcasing vegan Italian food, to be released in 2018. Sign up at thenomadicvegan.com/veganitaly to get advance access to the first chapter and be notified as soon as the book is published.

Vegano Italiano: 150 Vegan Recipes from the Italian Table. A recipe book by Rosalba Gioffré, originally released in Italian and now translated into English.

Nonna's Italian Kitchen: Delicious Home-Style Vegan Cuisine. A recipe book by vegan cooking expert Bryanna Clark Grogan, who presents regional Italian dishes and also delves into Italy's food history.

Vegan Italiano: Meat-free, Egg-free, Dairy-free Dishes from Sun-Drenched Italy. A cookbook by Donna Klein that focuses on whole foods and does not call for any meat or dairy substitutes.

Vegan Travel Club (formerly *Vegano Italiano Tours*). A vegan tour company that runs tours to southern Italy, accompanied by vegan celebrities such as vegan cheesemaker Miyoko Schinner.

Veg Jaunts and Journeys and I will be collaborating in 2018 to offer you a vegan tour of Italy. I will be leading this tour personally, and together we will visit the charming cities of Roma, Bologna and Lucca and discover the delicious vegan treasures of Italian cuisine.

Mexico and Mexican Food

The Lotus and the Artichoke ¡Mexico! A cookbook written and illustrated by Justin P. Moore, who combines stories of his own travels in Mexico with recipes that he learned from local cooks or concocted on his own from local ingredients while living in the Mexican seaside town of Lo de Marcos.

Vegan Mexico: Soul-Satisfying Regional Recipes from Tamales to Tostadas. A recipe book by Jason Wyrick that offers a deeper look into the history and traditions of

Mexican cooking, along with authentic regional recipes like "Oaxacan Black Beans" and "Sonoran Machaca Burritos".

Vegan Tacos: Authentic and Inspired Recipes for Mexico's Favorite Street Food. Also by Jason Wyrick, this book is devoted exclusively to Mexico's favorite antojito - the taco.

¡Salud! Vegan Mexican Cookbook: 150 Mouthwatering Recipes from Tamales to Churros. A new book by Eddie Garza, who combines innovative cooking techniques with traditional Mexican staples, creating recipes that are both delicious and healthy.

The Taco Cleanse: The Tortilla-Based Diet Proven to Change Your Life. A tongue-in-cheek parody of all the detoxes and cleanses on the market these days. The book contains 75 vegan taco recipes.

Viva Vegan!: 200 Authentic and Fabulous Recipes for Latin Food Lovers. A recipe book by Terry Hope Romero that covers every aspect of Latin cooking across the Americas, including a number of Mexican recipes.

Decolonize Your Diet: Plant-Based Mexican-American Recipes for Health and Healing. A lacto-ovo vegetarian cookbook by Luz Calvo and Catriona Rueda Esquibel, who encourage Mexicans to ditch the fast food and return to their own culture's food roots for both physical health and spiritual fulfillment.

Vegan Mexican Food. A website created by the *Food Empowerment Project* that features plant-based Mexican recipes that have been contributed by food lovers from all over the world.

Dora's Table. A recipe blog run by a Mexican woman named Dora who creates vegan Mexican recipes that stay true to traditional and regional Mexican cuisine. Dora has also written an ebook called Vegan Tamales Unwrapped.

The Middle East and Middle Eastern Food

One Arab Vegan. A blog run by Nada, who shares plant-based recipes inspired by Middle Eastern flavors and also writes about what it's like to be a vegan in the Arab world.

Chef in Disguise. A blog by Sawsan, who shares authentic Middle Eastern recipes and offers a glimpse into her life as a woman in the Middle East. Sawsan's blog does include non-vegan recipes, but she tags all of her vegan recipes so they are easy to find.

A Lebanese Feast of Vegetables, Pulses, Herbs and Spices. A vegetarian and mostly vegan recipe book by Mona Hamadeh, who grew up in Lebanon and now lives in England.

Vegetarian Dishes from Across the Middle East. A recently reprinted cookbook from 1983 that includes 250 authentic recipes that showcase the vibrant flavors and the healthy variety of plant-based Middle Eastern cooking.

Ahalan Olympus is an Israeli tour operator that offers a 10-day vegan tour of Israel.

Tel Aviv Vegan Food Tour takes you inside the booming vegan culture of Tel Aviv, Israel and helps you navigate the wide selection of vegan options there.

Morocco and Moroccan Food

Marrakech Day Trips. A tour company that offers a number of short day trips to sights in and around Marrakech, as well as longer desert tours lasting for up to four days. They understand veganism and can cater for vegan travelers.*Experience it Tours*. A US-based tour company that runs multi-day tours to Morocco and Tunisia and is also very aware of the needs of vegan travelers.

Vegetarian Tagines & Couscous: 60 Delicious Recipes for Moroccan One-Pot Cooking. A vegetarian recipe book by Ghillie Basan that includes many variations on Morocco's two most popular dishes - tajine and couscous. If you substitute the *smen* with olive oil or another plant-based oil, then most of the recipes are vegan.

Vegetarian Table: North Africa. A beautifully illustrated recipe book by Kitty Morse that includes vegetarian and vegan recipes from all the Maghreb countries, including many from Morocco.

Dinners and Dreams. A blog created by Nisrine Merzouki, a vegetarian Moroccan woman living in the United States. You will find recipes for vegan Moroccan dishes as well as other types of food on her blog.

Thailand and Thai Food

May Kaidee's Thai Vegetarian and Vegan Cookbook. A recipe book by vegetarian restaurateur and cooking instructor May Kaidee, who owns a chain of vegetarian restaurants in Thailand, Cambodia, and New York City. Cooking classes are also offered at the restaurant locations in Bangkok and Chiang Mai.

The Best of Vegetarian Thai Food. A cookbook of vegetarian Thai recipes by Sisamon Kongpan. It includes recipes for snacks, soups, one-plate dishes, salads, and mains.

Eating Thai Food. A blog written by Mark Wiens. While Mark is not vegan or vegetarian, he did complete a one-month vegetarian challenge while living in Bangkok, and during that time he wrote every day about all the different vegetarian dishes he ate there. Those daily blog posts are a great source of info on the types of veggie foods available in Thailand.

Vegan Food Quest. A vegan travel blog that focuses mostly on Southeast Asia and includes vegan destination guides covering Bangkok, Chiang Mai, and Koh Kood.

Vietnam and Vietnamese Food

The Viet Vegan - food blog run by a Vietnamese Canadian vegan, who shares Vietnamese recipes as well as recipes for other types of food. She also has recipe tutorial videos on her YouTube channel.

Vegan Vietnam - a great source of information about where to find delicious vegan food in Vietnam, including destination guides to specific towns and cities, as well as more general cultural tips.

Vegan Food Quest - a vegan travel blog that focuses mostly on Southeast Asia and includes vegan destination guides for Ho Chi Minh City, Hội An, Côn Đảo and Nha Trang.

Karma Waters is a vegan restaurant with branches in Hoi An and Danang, and they also run one-day vegan tours that include a homestay on the Cham Islands and an organic vegetable village tour.

Lịch Việt Nam (for iPhone) and *Lịch Việt* (for Android). Vietnamese calendar apps that will help you keep track of the Buddhist fasting days in Vietnam.

Acknowledgements

I owe a huge thanks to all the members of the Veggie Planet Street Team who gave helpful feedback and suggested ways of improving this book. Veggie Planet certainly would not be what it is today if it weren't for: Arielle Macey-Pilcher, Billie Abbitt, Caitlin Galer-Unit, Chris Karl, Cinzia Masoero, Colton Rowell, David Finney, Deborah Wicks, Emma Tamlyn, Erin Lucas, Geoff Leonard, Giulia Dentice, Janice Stanger, Jill Sarapata, Julia Feliz Brueck, Karlheinz Ulmer, Kati Reijonen, Kati Tímár, Kim Sujovolsky, Lacey Gaechter, Lani Muelrath, Mel Jackson, Marion Leonard, Maurice Michael Alvarez-Toye, Pat Gold, Rachida Brocklehurst, Renata Scotti, Robin Raven, Sam Anthony, Sarah Smith, Sharon Haberman, Tim Hordo, Vittoria Pasca, Vivian Penelope Alvéz, Yohana Genova, the Wanderlust Vegans, and Vegan Vietnam. Apologies if I have left anyone out. But if I have, thank you anyway. You surely know who you are.

And a very special thank you to Nick, my travel companion, personal chef, food photographer, video editor, best friend and life partner. Thank you for your patience and understanding on all the mornings when I holed myself up in the attic to work on this book.

Claim Your Free Gifts

If you have not yet claimed your free bonus package, just go to the link below to gain instant access to all the bonuses mentioned inside this book. The package includes:

- Three daily practices to create an abundance mindset
- Lists of non-vegan ingredients to avoid in each cuisine
- Downloadable pocket guides that you can take with you when eating out
- Full-color photos of the dishes described in Veggie Planet

To claim your free gifts, go to:

thenomadicvegan.com/veggieplanetbonuses

#1Book10Lives

Guess what? You just saved 10 lives! By purchasing this book, you spared 10 animals from a life of misery in industrial animal agriculture.

How? A portion of the proceeds from every book sold will be donated to The Humane League - an organization that works relentlessly to reduce animal suffering through grassroots education to change eating habits and corporate campaigns to reform farm animal treatment.

According to estimates published by Animal Charity Evaluators, the amount donated for each book sold is enough to spare the lives of 10 animals. Want to help me help MORE animals? Use the hashtag **#1Book10Lives** to spread the word!

Just share a photo or comment on Instagram or Twitter to tell people about the book, and about how they too can spare innocent lives just by purchasing a copy.

Not sure what to post? Don't worry, I've made it super easy by creating pre-written text and images for you, which you can find at thenomadicvegan.com/1-book-10-lives. All it takes is one click! Let's see how many animals we can help together!

One last thing ...

If you enjoyed this book and found it to be helpful, I would be extremely appreciative if you could take a minute to review it on Amazon. Reviews play a big role in the success of a book, and for independent authors like me they are crucial. I would really love to hear what you liked or didn't like about the book, so that I can improve my work in the future and be more effective in helping people enjoy the benefits of a vegan lifestyle. Thank you so much!

Sincerely,

Wendy Werneth

thenomadicvegan.com